# International Trade and
# Distortions in Factor Markets

# BUSINESS ECONOMICS AND FINANCE

*a series of monographs and textbooks*

*Executive Editor*
**Arthur B. Laffer**

Department of Economics
University of Chicago
Graduate School of Business
Chicago, Illinois

*Other Volumes in Preparation.*

# International Trade and Distortions in Factor Markets

STEPHEN P. MAGEE

*Graduate School of Business*
*University of Chicago*
*Chicago, Illinois*

MARCEL DEKKER, INC.    New York and Basel

MARCEL DEKKER, INC.
*270 Madison Avenue, New York, New York 10016*

LIBRARY OF CONGRESS CATALOG CARD NUMBER: 75-25163
ISBN: 0-8247-6339-4

Current printing (last digit):
10 9 8 7 6 5 4 3 2 1

*Printed in the United States of America*

To Nanneska

# Introduction

Among the principal major areas of analysis by the pure theorists of trade in the postwar literature, we must assign the central place to the theory of distortions, both in its positive and principally in its welfare aspects.

James Meade's early, seminal work on the theory of international economic policy extended to both the balance of payments (1951) and the pure-trade-theoretic (1955) issues. However, it was the former that had maximal impact, while the theory of distortions came into its own, by and large, quite independently of Meade's work and owed much to important papers such as Gottfried Haberler's (1950) celebrated *Economic Journal* article.

Indeed, in the nearly three decades since Haberler's 1950 analysis, the theory of market distortions in an open economy has been significantly enriched. In particular, the welfare theory of first- and second-best policy interventions in the presence of distortions has been mapped out and systematized: the principal landmarks since Haberler being the Bhagwati-Ramaswami (1963) analysis of domestic distortions [inspired, in turn, by Haberler and Hagen (1958)], the admirably lucid and cogent restatement of these results in Harry Johnson's (1965) influential Haberler *festschrift* contribution, and my subsequent (1971) synthesis of these and several other results into a generalized theory of distortions and welfare in the Kindleberger *festschrift*.

A principal component of the analysis of distortions has been the study of factor market distortions: whether "endogenous," market imperfections

or policy-imposed. Three principal "types" have been studied in the literature: (1) where the "shadow" wage differs from the actual wage: the "sticky
wage" problem; (2) where the wage is sticky but only in one of the sectors:
the "sector-specific, sticky wage" problem; and (3) where the wage is fully
flexible but is unequal between the sectors: the "wage differential" problem.
(The analysis of the Arthur Lewis (1954) type of factor market imperfection,
where wages are equal between sectors but equal the average product in one
sector, has not received the same degree of attention by trade theorists so far.)

The analysis of the *sticky wage* imperfection was initiated by Haberler
(1950) and pushed further by several theorists such as Harry Johnson (1965),
myself (1968), and Louis Lefeber (1971) until it culminated in the important
analysis of Richard Brecher (1974*a,b*).

The analysis of the *sector-specific sticky wage* problem was pioneered
by John Harris and Michael Todaro (1970); they investigated the problem
from the viewpoint of migration in a closed economy from the rural to the
urban sector when the latter (alone) has a minimum wage by legislation,
in a paper which is a classic in developmental theory. The generalization
of this problem of minimum wage to the sector-specificity of the sticky
wage and the analysis of alternative policy interventions in an open economy
has been undertaken by T. N. Srinivasan and Bhagwati (1974, 1976).

The *wage differential* problem, to which Stephen Magee's work is
addressed, was brought into the center of trade-theoretic analysis by Everett
Hagen's (1958) examination of it from the viewpoint of the desirability
of protection for the sector having to pay a higher wage for the same
factor. The focus on policy intervention, at the same time, implied that
trade theorists increasingly discovered "pathologies" in the presence of such
a wage differential. Hagen himself had noted that a nontangency would
characterize the equilibrium relationship between the price ratio and the
shrunk-in production possibility curve. However, Albert Fishlow and Paul
David (1961) further argued that the differential could remove the convexity
of the (feasible) production possibility set, prompting a somewhat more
ambitious assault on the problem by Harry Johnson (1966) and more success-
ful analysis of the conditions determining such a pathological outcome by
Herberg and Kemp (1971) and by Bhagwati and Srinivasan (1971). Yet
another pathology which was discovered was that output response to price
change could be perverse: and this, not merely in the rather obvious sense
that the output of a commodity would fall if its price rose, but in the more
subtle sense that the output could rise (fall) when price fell (rose) despite
convexity (concavity) of the production possibility set, the conditions again
being worked out for these alternative possibilities, for instance, in Bhagwati

and Srinivasan (1971). Another intriguing consequence of the differential noted there was that one could have two countries satisfying all the Samuelson conditions for factor price equalization in a 2 X 2 world, each have an identical wage differential in the same sector, and yet factor price equalization could break down: the unique relationship between commodity and factor prices no longer held.*

Magee's own contribution to this flood of intellectual activity was to be notable. His dissertation research threw much light on these issues, as will be evident to the reader of his 1971 *Quarterly Journal of Economics* paper and his joint paper with Kemp and Herberg in the 1971 *Economic Record*. Indeed, to the careful student of the subject, it will be clear that Magee's work influenced and/or overlapped with the thinking and research of many of the senior trade theorists who were working in this area at the time.

But Magee's published work was only the tip of the iceberg. His 1969 dissertation for the Massachusetts Institute of Technology carried the analysis of the effects of wage differentials in two principal directions: their structural effects (that is, on factor rewards, outputs, etc.) and their consequences for the principal theorems of international economics. Of interest in the former category is Magee's neat paradox that increasing the wage differential for labor in an activity will inevitably hurt labor if that activity is labor-intensive: a conclusion that should interest trade unions seeking wage increases. In regard to trade theory, Magee worked out the effects of introducing a wage differential on well-known propositions such as the Rybczynski theorem (it holds despite the differential: exogenous factor endowment augmentation increases output in the industry using the augmented factor intensively in the Samuelson sense and decreases output in the other industry), the Stolper-Samuelson theorem (it holds provided we shift from the Samuelson factor-intensity to the differential-weighted factor-intensity rankings) and the Heckscher-Ohlin theorem (where Magee mapped out the entire range of possibilities ingeniously with the aid of the Edgeworth-Bowley box diagram).

---

*It turns out that, for nearly all these pathologies, a critical factor in the outcome is whether, despite the assumption of Samuelson factor-intensity nonreversals, the ranking of factor-intensities *when weighted by the differential* reverses with the postulated change. Magee, following Jones, describes the Samuelson definition of factor-intensities as "physical" and the differential-weighted factor-intensity as "value"; this distinction, however, is better described in my view as simply (Samuelson) factor-intensity and differential-weighted factor-intensity. Either way, as is clear from the analysis in all the papers cited here, and was certainly noted clearly in Magee's dissertation (1969) as well, it is evident that the principal difficulties arise when, despite the (Samuelson) factor-intensity reversals being ruled out, the policy or parametric change in question leads to a reversal of the differential-weighted factor intensity between the two activities.

The present volume both draws on these and further results from the dissertation and extends them in yet other directions; it also brings together the results of innumerable other papers that have been written on the subject, integrating them with Magee's own impressive research. There are few interesting and even policy-relevant questions (for example, the effects of factor-taxes) that Magee has not thought of.

The result is that this volume represents a certain addition to the small list of books that must be read by every serious student of the pure theory of international trade. I have little doubt that it will also establish Magee, whose work on the empirical questions of trade is well-known, as a full-fledged member of the set of distinguished international economists that the Massachusetts Institute of Technology has produced over the last many years.

Jagdish N. Bhagwati

## References

Bhagwati, J. and V. K. Ramaswami, 1963, "Domestic Distortions, Tariffs and the Theory of Optimum Subsidy," *Journal of Political Economy, 71* (February), 44-50.

Bhagwati, J., 1968, *The Theory and Practice of Commercial Policy,* Frank Graham Memorial Lecture (1967), Special Papers in International Economics No. 8, Princeton University.

Bhagwati, J. and T. N. Srinivasan, 1971, "The Theory of Wage Differentials: Production Response and Factor Price Equalization," *Journal of International Economics, 1* (February), 19-35.

Bhagwati, J., 1971, "The Generalized Theory of Distortions and Welfare," in *Trade, Balance of Payments and Growth* (J. Bhagwati *et al.*, eds.), Papers in International Economics in Honor of Charles P. Kindleberger. Amsterdam: North Holland, pp. 69-90.

Bhagwati, J. and T. N. Srinivasan, 1974, "On Reanalyzing the Harris-Todaro Model: Policy Rankings in the Case of Sector-Specific Wages," *American Economic Review* (June), 502-508; MIT Working Paper No. 99, 1973.

Brecher, R., 1974*a*, "Minimum Wage Rates and the Pure Theory of International Trade," *Quarterly Journal of Economics* (February), 98-116.

Brecher, R., 1974*b*, "Optimum Commercial Policy for an Open Economy," *Journal of International Economics* (May), 139-150.

Fishlow, A. and P. A. David, 1961, "Optimal Resource Allocation in an Imperfect Market Setting," *Journal of Political Economy, 69* (December), 529-546.

Haberler, G., 1950, "Some Problems in the Pure Theory of International Trade," *Economic Journal, 60* (June), 223-240, reprinted in *Readings in*

*International Economics* (R. E. Caves and H. G. Johnson, eds.) Homewood, Illinois: Richard D. Irwin, 1968, pp. 213-229.

Hagen, E., 1958, "An Economic Justification of Protectionism," *Quarterly Journal of Economics, 72* (November), 496-514.

Harris, J. and M. Todaro, 1970, "Migration, Unemployment and Development: A Two-Sector Analysis," *American Economic Review* (March), 126-142.

Herberg, H. and M. Kemp, 1971, "Factor Market Distortions, the Shape of the Locus of Competitive Outputs and the Relation Between Product Prices and Equilibrium Outputs," in *Trade, Balance of Payments and Growth* (J. Bhagwati *et al.*, eds.), Papers in International Economics in Honor of Charles P. Kindleberger. Amsterdam: North Holland, pp. 22-48.

Herberg, H., M. Kemp, and S. P. Magee, 1971, "Factor Market Distortions, the Reversal of Relative Factor Intensities, and the Relation Between Product Prices and Equilibrium Outputs," *Economic Record, 47* (December), 518-530.

Johnson, H. G., 1965, "Optimal Trade Intervention in the Presence of Domestic Distortions," in *Trade, Growth and the Balance of Payments* (R. Baldwin *et al.*) Amsterdam: North Holland, pp. 3-34.

Johnson, H. G., 1966, "Factor Market Distortions and the Shape of the Transformation Curve," *Econometrica, 34* (July), 686-698.

Jones, R. W., 1971, "Distortions in Factor Markets and the General Equilibrium Model of Production," *Journal of Political Economy, 79* (May/June), 437-459.

Lefeber, L., 1971, "Trade and Minimum Wage Rates," in *Trade, Balance of Payments and Growth* (J. Bhagwati *et al.*, eds.) Amsterdam: North Holland.

Lewis, W. A., 1954, "Economic Development with Unlimited Supplies of Labour," in *The Economics of Underdevelopment* (A. N. Agarwala and S. P. Singh, eds.) New York: Oxford University Press, 1963, pp. 400-449. Reprinted from *The Manchester School, 22* (May 1954), pp. 139-191.

Magee, S. P., 1969, "Factor Market Distortions and the Pure Theory of International Trade," unpublished Ph.D. dissertation, Massachusetts Institute of Technology (May).

Magee, S. P., 1971, "Factor Market Distortions, Production, Distribution and the Pure Theory of International Trade," *Quarterly Journal of Economics, 75* (November), 623-643.

Magee, S. P., 1973, "Factor Market Distortions, Production and Trade: A Survey," *Oxford Economic Papers, 25* (March), 1-43.

Meade, J. E., 1951, *Trade and Welfare.* London: Oxford University Press.

Meade, J. E., 1955, *Trade and Welfare.* London: Oxford University Press.

Srinivasan, T. N. and J. Bhagwati, 1976, "Alternative Policy Rankings in a Large, Open Economy with Sector-Specific Wages," *Journal of Economic Theory,* forthcoming; MIT Economics Working Paper No. 109, May 1973.

# Preface

This book is a revision of my Ph.D. dissertation, submitted to the Department of Economics at the Massachusetts Institute of Technology in May 1969. For years, $2 \times 2$ trade theory had operated in what I felt was a theoretical vacuum: all of the standard theorems included the assumption of "no imperfections in factor markets." The purpose of my dissertation was to examine each of these theorems (Heckscher-Ohlin, Stolper-Samuelson, Rybczynski, Samuelson-Johnson, etc.) to find when they do and do not hold when we relax the assumption of perfect factor markets. In effect, the goal was to examine standard general equilibrium trade theory at *all* points in the Edgeworth-Bowley box and not just along the traditional nondistorted efficiency locus. The purpose of this book is to provide students of trade and factor market theory with a survey of the results, both from my own work and from that of others. The methodological tool used in my work is the factor price differential; e.g., labor or capital in one industry receives a constant proportion above or below the return to the same factor in another industry. The work here analyzes the general equilibrium effects of this behavior. Factor price differentials have empirical counterparts which make these results useful; "pattern setting" of wages by unions across industries (which do not reflect differential skill) is an obvious example. We find, surprisingly, that labor may make itself worse off in both industries (including the high-wage industry) by such a strategy: even apart from the unemployment which accompanies all short-run adjustment processes, labor may receive a lower real wage in all industries in the long run.

A number of intellectual debts should be acknowledged. I am grateful to the members of my dissertation committee, Charles Kindleberger, Paul Samuelson, and especially to Jagdish Bhagwati for guidance and assistance. Harry Johnson deserves thanks for his article on distortions, "Factor Market Distortions and the Shape of the Transformation Curve," *Econometrica* (1966), which stimulated my interest in their structural effects. In the fall of 1969, while teaching at the University of California at Berkeley, I received helpful comments from Ronald Jones, Murray Kemp, and Richard Caves, all of whom were in residence. In December 1969, I presented the paper which later appeared in 1971 in the *Quarterly Journal of Economics* at the Seminar in International Economics at Berkeley. There, Ronald Jones made several helpful suggestions, including the economic interpretation of $k_x - k_y$ and $k_y - tk_x$ as physical and value factor intensities; I also learned several things from the article which he subsequently wrote for the *Journal of Political Economy*, 1971, "Distortions in Factor Markets and the General Equilibrium Model of Production." Murray Kemp was the Ford Foundation Visiting Research Scholar at Berkeley in 1969-1970; I benefited from discussions with him and from our joint authorship with Horst Herberg of a paper, "Factor Market Distortions, the Reversal of Relative Factor Intensities, and the Relation Between Product Prices and Equilibrium Outputs," which appeared in the *Economic Record* in 1971. I have also benefited from comments by Max Corden and Carlos Rodriguez.

I would like to thank Arthur Laffer, the economics editor of this series, and Gene Uselton for encouraging me to publish this in the series, with special thanks to the editor for his patience while I was revising the book. Part of the dissertation has already appeared in print. I am indebted to the *Quarterly Journal of Economics* for allowing me to include portions of "Factor Market Distortions, Production, Distribution and the Pure Theory of International Trade," which appeared in November 1971, and to the *Oxford Economic Papers* for permission to use material from "Factor Market Distortions, Production and Trade: A Survey," which appeared in March 1973. These papers are not included here as individual chapters. Results from the former study appear here in Chaps. 2, 3, and 4; results from the latter are scattered throughout Chaps. 1 to 6.

The figures and diagrams for this book were done by Donna Marder, the indexes were compiled by Patti Pazera, and Carol Nackenoff provided research assistance. I am grateful to the following for financial assistance along the way: the Woodrow Wilson National Fellowship Foundation; the Institute of International Studies at Berkeley; the Graduate School of Business, University of Chicago; the National Science Foundation; and, most importantly, to my wife, Nan, for putting me through graduate school. This book belongs to her.

# Contents

# International Trade and
# Distortions in Factor Markets

# 1
## Differentials and Distortions: Types and Causes

The traditional interest of economists in monopoly power and other distortions in product markets has shifted in recent years toward the problem of distortions and differentials in factor markets. This book reviews and extends the literature in this area and emphasizes the implications of factor distortions for the 2 X 2 pure theory of international trade. General studies which include at least brief discussions of factor market imperfections have been written by Bhagwati [20], Caves [43], Corden [47], Johnson [104], Linder [136], Myint [173], Taussig [222], and Viner [237]. We do not consider here issues in the controversy over the theory of capital (see Harcourt's survey [83]).

Important theoretical papers on the subject should be mentioned. Four early works are by Cairnes [41], Manoilesco [146], Ohlin [176], and Viner [235]. While Stolper and Samuelson [217] do not deal with distortions per se, their study of factor rewards in general equilibrium provides an important analytical tool in this area. In the 1950s, Eckaus [53], Haberler [73], Hagen [75], and Lewis [135] wrote on the subject, while Bhagwati and Ramaswami [24], Bhagwati et al. [25], Fishlow and David [60], Johnson [104, 105], Johnson and Mieszkowski [110], and the present author [140] studied the problem in the 1960s. Since 1969, there has been an explosion of theoretical and empirical papers on the subject.

One of the most interesting early papers on distortions is the study written by Ohlin [175] in 1931 in which he reviews Manoilesco's book [146]; it is interesting because it develops verbally several of the conclusions which have been developed mathematically by the modern writers. A comprehensive modern treatment of the welfare effects is by Bhagwati [23], who has formulated a general theory encompassing the three causes and four possible types of economic distortions (factor market distortions being only one of the four).

Following Bhagwati [21], we can expand the traditional definition of a differential to incorporate two types. First, factor prices may be the same in all industries but there may exist a differential between real factor rewards and their marginal products in one or more industries. Second, real factor rewards may equal their respective marginal products in each industry but there may be a differential between the price of an identical factor in different industries. This expanded definition of a differential will thus incorporate more than one of the various inequalities which may arise in the factor market equilibrium conditions.

The word "differential" is used here as a positive or purely descriptive term, while "distortion" denotes that a differential has either normative or welfare implications (see Bhagwati and Ramaswami [24]). In the present context, a distortion can be related to a differential, but not every differential implies that a distortion exists. Thus, a differential is a necessary but not a sufficient condition for a distortion.

For example, many studies have found factor price differentials which do not necessarily indicate distortion. The differentials may be caused by differences in the following:

1.  Age and experience among workers in Refs. 1, 76, 81, 103, 125, 164
2.  Education and skill reflecting a return on human capital in Refs. 1, 3, 24, 76, 81, 98, 102, 103, 113, 125, 164, 175, 182, 189, 202
3.  Moving costs and related factors in Refs. 24, 32, 68, 80, 81, 147, 208, 243

4. Factor preference or disutility associated with particular industries or regions in Refs. 1, 60, 73, 90, 104, 175, 235, 236
5. Risk aversion in Ref. 59
6. Geographic concentration of low wage-low skill industries in Refs. 66, 80

On the other hand, a large number of differentials have been cited, sometimes incorrectly, as sources of welfare distortion. The causes of these differentials include the following:

1. Imperfect knowledge in Refs. 53, 60
2. The rural-urban dichotomy in Ref. 75
3. Racism in Refs. 16, 35, 177, 223, 243
4. Monopoly power through unionism in Refs. 2, 24, 46, 105, 110, 134, 139, 159, 175, 184, 198, 202, 209, 224, 227
5. Monopoly power by one or both factors coupled with market power by producers in product markets (bilateral monopoly) in Refs. 2, 8, 34, 82, 83, 95, 191, 198, 204
6. The maintenance and spread of union wage increases by "pattern setting" in Refs. 138, 204
7. Seniority based on age or education which does not reflect economic superiority in Refs. 1, 103, 125, 243
8. Differences between the export and import-competing sectors' access to foreign capital in Ref. 49, or differences in ocean freight rates charged to the two sectors in Ref. 149
9. Discrimination against women or children in Refs. 21, 103, 125, 243
10. Collusion across industries by a factor which acts as a discriminating monopolist, charging different prices in each industry because of differing elasticities of derived demand for the factor in Ref. 198
11. Disguised unemployment in agriculture relative to manufacturing in Refs. 24, 105, 135
12. Differential factor taxation or subsidy in Refs. 103, 104, 125, 161, 197

13.  Factory legislation, social regulation, or policy control for "prestige-cum-humanitarian" or other normative reasons in Refs. 24, 26, 53

14.  Movements in union/nonunion differentials in the business cycle in Refs. 179, 184, 224

15.  Limited mobility with differential product growth in Refs. 75, 105, 146

In Bhagwati's terminology [23], the first eleven types are caused by "endogenous forces" while types 12 and 13 are "policy imposed"; all thirteen are distortionary in a static context, while types 14 and 15 involve both a distortion and comparative statics, raising the possibility of immiserizing growth. Further, in dynamic systems, differentials may be observed during the adjustment process between two equilibrium points.

Differentials, regardless of their cause, have two major effects: The first is on the economic *structure* while the second is on *welfare*. The structural effects can be analyzed independently of whether the differential is distortionary, ceteris paribus. Bhagwati has suggested the following classification of the structural effects of a differential:

(i)    The *output* effects

(ii)   The *shrinkage* of the production possibilities curve due to operation off the efficiency locus in capital-labor space

(iii)  *Nontangency,* i.e., nonequivalence of the marginal rates of transformation and substitution in product space

(iv)   *Convexity,* i.e., the possibility that the production possibilities curve becomes convex to the origin because of the differential

(v)    The *factor market* effects, including possible reversal of the product factor intensities

(vi)   The *trade* effects

(For convenience, these effects will be referred to in the text only by the word which is italicized.) The welfare and policy implications of a differential depend on whether it is distortionary. In the cases considered in this book, we assume that the differential causes a distortion so that the words "differential" and "distortion" are used interchangeably. While one-factor models are considered, most of the analysis pertains to two-factor models in which we make the traditional assumptions of two factors in fixed total supply and immobile internationally, two goods, perfect competition in both product and factor markets, increasing opportunity costs between the two products, constant returns to scale in production, and no externalities. The assumption of perfect factor markets, in which factor prices are flexible and identical across industries and the factors are perfectly mobile between industries, will be relaxed in what follows.

The most widely discussed cause of factor market distortions is the case in which factors are relatively mobile and their prices flexible and yet a differential exists in the price of a factor in different industries. This case is not always clearly distinguishable from the case in which there is some factor immobility. For example, labor unions frequently exploit their monopoly power by a combination of price setting and restricted entry, the latter introducing a form of immobility.

Differentials may be observed in static or comparative static systems and in systems in the dynamic adjustment process between two equilibria. We noted earlier a number of causes of nondynamic differentials. We shall discuss briefly the *dynamic* variety. They are more difficult to classify as distortions since the size of the differential depends on the time period chosen, the speed of convergence (assuming stability), the size of the initial shock, and how recently the system was jolted by an exogenous change. The dynamic differential is another case of partial factor mobility in which adjustment to change is not instantaneous. A nonexplosive cobweb model with lagged supply and demand reactions generates an observable differential if the period of observation is small and no differential if the observation period is sufficiently long. Hagen's [75] use of more rapid demand expansion for manufactures than for agriculture to generate a factor distortion has been criticized by Kenen [121], Koo [125], Fishlow and David [60], and Bhagwati and Ramaswami [24] as "illegitimately superimposing a dynamic argument upon a comparative statics framework" [24, p. 48].

Recent papers, following Inada [101] and Uekawa [225], have explored growth models in which one factor (Herberg [90]) or all factors (Herberg and Kemp [92]) are imperfectly mobile. This allows generation of endogenous differentials, which disappear in the steady state. The empirical question of growth with regional income differentials has been analyzed by Fukuchi [67] for Japan.

One can identify both demand-induced differentials and cost-induced differentials, generated by sectoral shifts in either the demand for or supply of particular factors (with the other factor being less than perfectly elastic). Regardless of the initial cause, the disparity in prices will not remain a permanent differential unless economic or noneconomic forces act to maintain it. For example, Schlesinger [204] has attributed union success to its alteration of the labor supply function; consequently, "excessive" wage demands would classify unionization as a cost-induced differential. But the union differential cannot be maintained indefinitely without other economic forces operating. One such force might be restricted entry through queuing. The differential received by labor in a unionized industry would cause an excess supply of labor willing to work in the unionized industry. The ex ante supply of labor in the unionized sector would be reduced to the demand for unionized labor by queuing. Such queuing techniques are administered through nepotism rules (first in line would be relatives of existing union members), "friend of a friend" rules, etc.

Examples of demand-induced differentials include discrimination by employers according to the race, sex, or age of prospective or existing employees. Employers who successfully employ minority races, women, or teenagers at wages below the existing rates for other workers of comparable quality are able to expand their output beyond levels which would exist in the absence of such negative factor price differentials. But the question arises: Why do laborers who are discriminated against not move into other sectors of the economy and eliminate the interindustry wage differentials? As before, there must be other economic or noneconomic forces acting to prevent the arbitrage process from working.

There are situations in which differentials can persist without requiring the ancillary assumptions just noted. For example, differentials caused by factor taxation in certain sectors (such as the corporate income tax) cause the factors of production to equalize the net of tax returns across all industries. The differential facing employers simply equals the tax.

In short, one should examine very carefully the way in which a differential is introduced, whether it is narrowing through the traditional dynamic adjustment process and if not, what, if any, conditions are required to maintain it. More systematic analyses should be done on the *policy* implications of the time dimension, such as the present discounted costs of dynamic endogenous differentials and the stability properties of tax-cum-subsidy policies designed to close endogenous differentials more rapidly.

We turn now from differentials caused by dynamic forces to static models in which differentials are largely exogenous to the system. In the next chapter we shall examine static differentials in both one- and two-factor models.

# The Output and Factor Market Effects of Factor Price Differentials

## 2.1 Differentials in One-Factor Models

The earliest works on factor price differentials dealt primarily with the Ricardian case of only one factor—labor (see, for example, Cairnes [41], Taussig [222], Ohlin [176], Viner [235], and Hagen [75]). Hagen [75, pp. 504-505] presents the best discussion of the one-factor, two-good model. One of his diagrams is reproduced in Fig. 2.1. The transformation curve BC is linear because of the one-factor, constant returns assumption. With no distortion, the economy will produce and consume at A in autarky. Introduce a differential such that wages in X are double those in Y. The domestic price ratio $P_x/P_y$ will then equal, except for sign, the slope of BC′, which is twice as steep as BC. This can be formalized as follows. Assuming internal solutions and using the fixed coefficient production functions $X = aL_x$ and $Y = bL_y$, profit maximization yields the first-order conditions $P_x = w_x/a$ and $P_y = w_y/b$, where $w_x$ and $w_y$ are the wages in X and Y. Thus,

$$\frac{P_x}{P_y} = \frac{w_x}{w_y}\left[\frac{b}{a}\right]$$

(2.1)

Without distortion, $w_x/w_y = 1$, but when we double $w_x/w_y$, then $P_x/P_y$ doubles. Thus, the original price ratio along BC in Fig. 2.1

9

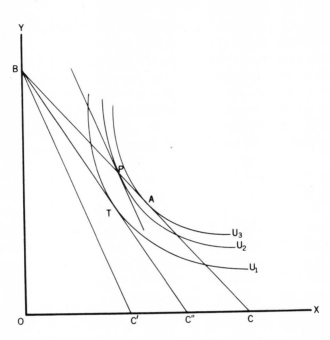

**FIG. 2.1.** Product market equilibria with a differential in the one factor model.

is [b/a], while the slope of a price line such as BC′ is 2[b/a].

In the absence of trade, the economy will produce and consume at P when the distortion is present. At that point, the marginal rate of substitution, which equals the price ratio corresponding to the slope of BC′, does not equal the marginal rate of transformation (the slope of BC). If the country initiates trade and faces a fixed international terms of trade, slope BC″, which lies between the slopes of BC and BC′, the country will specialize in Y, will export Y, and will consume at T (which in this case is inferior to both P and A). The country produces only Y since the autarky relative price of X (the slope of the price line tangent to $U_2$ at P) exceeds the world relative price of X (the slope of BC′). Hagen was using this analysis, in fact, to show that protectionism can be superior to free trade, i.e., that the utility level at P with a prohibitive tariff is superior to the free trade level at T.

Notice that the pattern of trade also depends on the size and direction of the differential. If the distorted domestic price ratio had been less than the international terms of trade (slope BC″), then the country would have specialized in X rather than Y. Using the formula developed above, we can say, in general, that if $(P_x/P_y)_I$ denotes the international terms of trade,

$$\left(\frac{P_x}{P_y}\right)_I \gtrless \frac{w_x}{w_y}\left[\frac{b}{a}\right] \tag{2.2}$$

implies specialization in X or Y, respectively. Clearly, $w_x/w_y$ can be manipulated by the differential to cause specialization either way. In summary, the differential reduces output of the industry paying the differential, causes nontangency and with international trade, it can reverse the pattern of trade.

Models with one factor and more than two products were discussed by Cairnes [41] in his controversy with the classicists. If labor is divided into noncompeting groups with each group aligned with a specific product, Cairnes argued that wage differentials will be determined exclusively by the demand for each product. Taussig [222, pp. 53-54] criticized Cairnes for ignoring the long-run supply response of labor (e.g., reproduction would increase within each noncompeting group whenever its wages rose above the subsistence level). Taussig [222, p. 57] went so far as to argue that international trade "is not likely to modify the alignment of grades [of labor] within a country," although that alignment could certainly affect international trade, as in his cases of pre-World War I German chemical exports and U.S. iron and steel exports. Taussig showed that the classical explanation of the pattern of trade still holds if the structure of relative wage distortions is the same between countries.

Samuelson [201] has discussed comparative advantage in a one-factor, many-good model without wage distortion. An explanation of the pattern of trade in the one-factor model with wage distortion can be developed using the Mangoldt-Edgeworth technique discussed by Viner [237, pp. 458-462]. We shall consider only two countries. The technique is general enough to consider cases in which both the level and structure of wages differ by country; here, however, we are interested only in the structural aspects. Even in the structural case, we are oversimplifying since the level of wages is determined partly by the reciprocal demand of the two countries for each other's products. We noted earlier that the cost of good i in a multiproduct, one-factor model can be written

$$P_i = \frac{w_i}{a_i} \qquad i = 1, \ldots, n \tag{2.3}$$

where $a_i$ represents the constant output-labor ratio and $w_i$ represents the wage paid by industry i. Assume initially that there are no factor price distortions so that $w_i$ is the same for all industries and that there are $n = 5$ industries. We can plot the logarithms of $P_1, \ldots, P_5$ for country I from a fixed point 0 in Fig. 2.2a on the left side of the line. Similarly the logarithms of prices $P_1, \ldots, P_5$ for country II, measured from the same point $0'$, are plotted on the right side of the line in Fig. 2.2. [If the wage levels in country II are greater (less) than those in I, $0'$ will lie above (below) 0; this was ruled out by assumption.] We can now determine which products will be exported by each country. Since the costs in country II of goods 1, 2, and 3 are lower and those of 4 and 5 are higher in Fig. 2.2a, then country II exports the former and country I exports the latter.

The Mangoldt-Edgeworth diagram can be used to show that when wage differentials are introduced, it is possible to obtain almost any pattern of trade. For example, if the relative wages in country II of goods 1, 2, and 3 are increased and those of 4 and 5 fall with the introduction of the differentials, then the pattern of trade can be reversed as in Fig. 2.2b. The same analysis could have been performed using Eq. (2.3). This analysis also illustrates Taussig's point that if the wage distortions are the same between countries, the pattern of trade is unaffected.

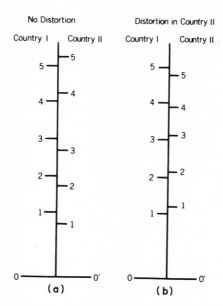

FIG. 2.2. Product prices with and without distortions in the Mangoldt-Edgeworth diagram.

## 2.2  Differentials in Two-Factor Models

Two important theoretical articles on the structural effects of factor price differentials were published by Harberger [82] and Johnson [105]. Harberger's paper was concerned exclusively with the incidence of the U.S. corporate income tax, and was followed by a study by Mieszkowski [161]. After some delay, Johnson's paper stimulated an avalanche of research on the mathematical properties of general equilibrium models in which factor price differentials are present. At least six theoretical papers were written independently in the late 1960s which explored factor price differentials and their effects on various properties of an economic system (Bhagwati and Srinivasan [27], Herberg and Kemp [91], Johnson and Mieszkowski [110], Lloyd [137], Magee [140], and Mundlak [172]). While each paper was concerned with slightly different problems, there was virtual unanimity on results when

identical problems were tackled. These papers elicited others by
Batra and Pattanaik [14], Herberg et al. [94], and Jones [112].
We turn now to an analysis of the factor market effects of a single
factor price differential in the 2 X 2 model.

The first five equations of the model to be developed here are
formally the same as those of Johnson [105, p. 690]. They contain
the two production functions, an endowment constraint, and two
first-order conditions for competitive factor market equilibrium in
the two industries. The subsequent equations specify domestic
income, domestic product demand, and domestic and foreign
product market equilibrium.

The two outputs X and Y are produced by the production
functions

$$X = F(K_x, L_x)$$
$$Y = G(K_y, L_y)$$

in which K and L are the amounts of capital and labor used in
production. If we assume that the production functions are linearly
homogeneous, a proportional change of both inputs results in an
equal proportional change in outputs. Let this proportional change
equal the multiplicative factor $1/L_i$ for industry i; then,

$$\frac{X}{L_x} = F\left(\frac{K_x}{L_x}, 1\right)$$
$$\frac{Y}{L_y} = G\left(\frac{K_y}{L_y}, 1\right)$$

These equations can be rewritten

$$X = L_x f(k_x)$$
$$Y = L_y g(k_y)$$

where $k_i = (K/L)_i$ is the capital-labor ratio and $L_i$ is the amount of
labor in industry i. We assume that both capital and labor are fully
employed and in fixed total supply, so that

$$L = L_x + L_y$$

$$K = K_x + K_y$$

with $L$ and $K$ denoting the country's total endowments of each. Using these endowment constraints, dividing both production functions by total labor $L$, and writing $x = X/L$, $y = Y/L$, we can rewrite the production functions

$$x = hf(k_x) \tag{2.4}$$

$$y = (1 - h)g(k_y) \tag{2.5}$$

where $h$ is the proportion of the total labor force in industry $X$. Dividing the capital endowment equation by $L$ and rearranging yields

$$k = hk_x + (1 - h)k_y \tag{2.6}$$

where $k$ is the country's total capital-labor ratio. Thus, $k$ is fixed and is a weighted average of the capital-labor ratios in the two industries with the weights equal to the shares of labor in each industry. If the reader feels uneasy about the use of the term "capital" here with its attendant complexities completely ignored, then he should substitute the word "land" for "capital." All units of labor and capital are of identical quality.

We consider next factor allocation in the two perfectly competitive industries $X$ and $Y$ (there are no distortions in product markets). A distortion is introduced in factor markets by assuming that the cost of capital to industry $X$ is a proportion $t$ of the cost of capital to industry $Y$. The choice of capital is purely arbitrary: the effects of differing labor costs between $X$ and $Y$ could be analyzed by a simple switching of the names of the factors. The assumption that a factor price in one industry can be fixed at a constant proportion of the price of the same factor in the other industry appears implausible at first sight. However, "pattern setting" of wages by unions for similar labor in different industries is an important empirical counterpart to this assumption of fixed factor price differentials. If $X$ pays 20% more for capital than $Y$, then $t = 1.20$ and the proportional excess of capital costs in X equals $t - 1$ or 0.20. In general, the price of capital to industry X is greater than, equal to, or less than the price to Y depending on whether t is greater than, equal to, or less than 1. The parameter t is positive. Let $P_x$ and $P_y$ represent the prices of output, and let w and r represent the prices of labor and capital to industry Y. Profit maximization by producers in both industries yields the following first-order conditions (primed variables denote first derivatives):

$$P_x f' = tr$$

$$P_x(f - k_x f') = w$$

$$P_y g' = r$$

$$P_y(g - k_y g') = w$$

where f and g are outputs per man in the two industries, $f'$ and $g'$ are the marginal products of capital, and $(f - k_x f')$ and $(g - k_y g')$ are the marginal products of labor in the X and Y industries, respectively. Eliminating w and r and letting $P = P_y/P_x$, we can reduce these equations to

$$\frac{f - k_x f'}{g - k_y g'} = P \tag{2.7}$$

$$\frac{f'}{g'} = tP \tag{2.8}$$

which complete the conditions for factor market equilibrium.

Some comments are in order regarding t. First, we are not assuming that wages and rental rates are inflexible but only that industry X pays a given differential $t - 1$ for capital relative to Y. Indeed, flexibility of w and r is necessary for the adjustment of the system to exogenous changes. Second, the factor market distortion just considered implies that the economy is not on its efficiency locus in the Edgeworth-Bowley box. The factor market distortion implied by Eqs. (2.7) and (2.8) is apparent when $t \neq 1$ since

$X_K/Y_K = tX_L/Y_L$. If, however, industry X also paid a differential $t - 1$ for labor relative to Y, the economy would not operate off the efficiency locus since $X_L/Y_L = tP = X_K/Y_K$, although there would be a divergence in product space between the marginal rate of transformation $dY/dX$ and the marginal rate of substitution along the transformation curve. Thus, while it is possible to have differentials in factor costs between industries without having factor market distortion, that case will not be considered until Chap. 3.

Let us extend the implications of the last two equations. Combining Eqs. (2.7) and (2.8) and eliminating P, we can write the ratios of the marginal products of capital to labor in both industries in the form

$$\frac{f'}{f - k_x f'} = t\left[\frac{g'}{g - k_y g'}\right] \tag{2.9}$$

where the left side of the equation represents (except for sign) the slope of the X isoquants in Fig. 2.3 and the bracketed term on the right side equals the slope of the Y isoquants. In this model, the nondistorted factor market is simply the special case in which $t = 1$, and corresponds to the traditional efficiency locus $X_0 SY_0$, where the slope of the X isoquant is steeper than that of the Y isoquant, as at point A in Fig. 2.3; there, the X industry pays relatively more for capital than Y. The converse holds below $X_0 SY_0$, as at point B. Each of the dashed lines in Fig. 2.3 represents a "distorted efficiency locus," or a "distorted contract curve." They are loci of points along which the slopes of the two production isoquants are the same (i.e., the value of t is constant). These loci first appeared in a paper by Johnson and Mieszkowski [110]. Marquez-Ruarte [148] has succinctly labeled them "iso-distortion loci;" we shall follow his nomenclature in what follows. We assume in Fig. 2.3 that factor intensities in the value sense (to be discussed later) are not reversed. The constant value of t along the diagonal is of special interest since it represents the factor reversal value of t; for all values of $t > t_r$, the original physical factor intensities of the two products are reversed since $k_x$ is less than k. These reversals should not be confused with those caused by different product

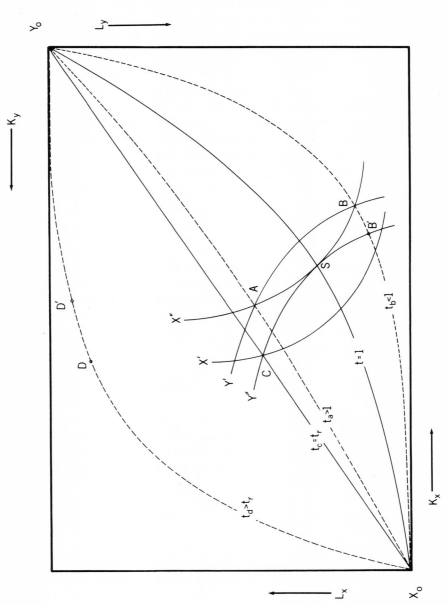

FIG. 2.3. Iso-distortion loci.

elasticities of substitution (which occur at identical relative factor prices). Note that the traditional definition of relative factor intensity must be relaxed in the distortion case since the two industries do not face the same relative factor price ratios. Physical factor intensities are defined here by the *observed* $k_x$ and $k_y$. Finally, the value of t is constant along the diagonal because of the homogeneity assumption. Once the value of the distortion parameter t has been specified at some value, say $t_a$, then we know that the factor market equilibrium will occur somewhere along the corresponding iso-distortion locus $X_0 A Y_0$.

The last six equations in the model specify income, domestic demand, product market equilibrium, and international equilibrium. Total real income per laborer, i = I/L, is defined as

$$i = x + Py \qquad (2.10)$$

and is expressed in terms of good X. For convenience, we will simply write the final consumer demand functions for X and Y consumed per laborer, $x^c$ and $y^c$, as functions of aggregate income and relative prices:

$$x^c = x^c(i,P) \qquad (2.11)$$

$$y^c = y^c(i,P) \qquad (2.12)$$

Notice that Eqs. (2.11) and (2.12) are reduced-form equations derived from utility maximization by consumers. They were derived by assuming that each individual maximized his utility with respect to his consumption of X and Y subject to his budget constraint:

$$\max U = U(x^c, y^c)$$
$$\text{s.t. } i = x^c + Py^c \qquad (2.13)$$

This maximization process yields the following first-order conditions:

$$\frac{u_y}{u_x} = \frac{1}{P} \tag{2.14}$$

$$i = x^c + Py^c \tag{2.15}$$

in which $u_i$ is the partial derivative of the utility function with respect to argument i. Given some reasonable restrictions on the form of the utility functions (see Samuelson [199]), Eqs. (2.14) and (2.15) can be solved explicitly for $x^c$ and $y^c$ as functions of i and P, yielding the demand functions in Eqs. (2.11) and (2.12).

Notice that Eq. (2.14) specifies that the slope of the utility isoquant U in Fig. 2.4 be tangent to the budget line $L_1$. The slope of $L_1$ is equal to the terms on both sides of Eq. (2.14), except for sign. The intercept of $L_1$ on the X axis equals income per laborer, i, in Eq. (2.15) times the labor force.

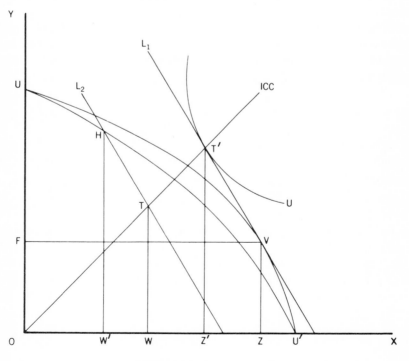

**FIG. 2.4.** Production, consumption, and trade.

If X is the export good and Y is the import-competing good in the absence of distortion (t = 1), we can write the product market equilibrium conditions

$$x^c = x - e \tag{2.16}$$

$$y^c = y + m \tag{2.17}$$

where e = E/L and m = M/L are exports and imports per man. Finally, the balance of payments equilibrium condition is

$$e = Pm \tag{2.18}$$

The model is simplified if we assume initially that the country does not possess monopoly power in international trade so that relative product prices are determined in world markets. Further, assume that the country is initially in free-trade equilibrium with product prices and factor prices equal to those abroad, and rule out problems such as transport costs and factor intensity reversals of the Minhas variety [165].

The model is not inconsistent in that we have ten independent equations [(2.4) through (2.8), (2.10) through (2.12), and (2.16) through (2.18)] in ten unknowns (x, y, $k_x$, $k_y$, h, i, $x^c$, $y^c$, m, e) and three parameters (k, t, P). Only ten of the eleven equations are independent since Eq. (2.18) can be derived from Eqs. (2.10) through (2.12), (2.16), and (2.17).

## 2.3 Physical and Value Factor Intensities

The traditional definition of a commodity's relative factor intensity is its relative capital-labor ratio measured at equivalent relative factor prices. However, this criterion is a special case of the definitions to be used here; it applies only to factor intensities in the absence of distortion. As factor price differentials change the relative prices of the factors to the two industries, by definition, the relative factor intensities change. Thus, in what follows, we shall define factor intensities to be the observed capital-labor ratios (or relative factor shares) for a specified price, endowment, and factor price differential. This leads to a second point.

An important distinction must be made between two types of factor intensities: *physical* factor intensities and *value* factor intensities. This distinction was not important in the pre-factor market distortion literature since the two intensities always correspond along the non-distorted efficiency locus in the Edgeworth-Bowley box. However, the distinction is important for the results in all other parts of the box. For that reason, some pains will be taken to develop the definitions of the two factor intensities and their properties (see Jones [112]).

Let PH represent the physical definition of relative factor intensity, i.e., the difference in the capital-labor ratios in the two industries:

$$PH \equiv k_y - k_x \qquad\qquad\qquad\qquad (2.19)$$

$< 0 \to$ X is physical capital intensive

$> 0 \to$ Y is physical capital intensive

The value factor intensity relates the two products in terms of the shares of the value of output in each industry going to each factor, i.e.,

$$VA \equiv \frac{r_y K_y}{w_y L_y} - \frac{r_x K_x}{w_x L_x}$$

$$\equiv \left(\frac{r}{w}\right)_y k_y - \frac{(r/w)_x}{(r/w)_y} k_x$$

$$\equiv \left(\frac{r}{w}\right)_y (k_y - t k_x) \qquad\qquad\qquad (2.20)$$

$< 0 \to$ X is value capital intensive

$> 0 \to$ Y is value capital intensive

The industry with the largest share of the value of output going to capital is said to be capital intensive in the value sense. The equations illustrate that, in the special case of no factor market distortions ($t = 1$), the value factor intensities and the physical factor intensities correspond: The industry with the greatest relative use of physical capital per man in production also has the largest share of output being paid to capital. From Eqs. (2.19) and (2.20), VA = $(r/w)_y$ PH. Since the signs of VA and PH must be the same in this case, the two correspond. When they are of opposite sign, a product is relatively capital intensive according to one definition and labor intensive according to the other. We now turn to some properties of physical and value factor intensity reversals.

Johnson [105] has noted that, if an industry pays a differential for its physically intensive factor, the *physical* factor intensities of the products can reverse. If production isoquants are homothetic, the differential t must exceed the (fixed) ratio of the slopes of the X to the Y isoquants along the diagonal in the Edgeworth-Bowley box (e.g., the relative slopes at point R in Fig. 2.5). We shall denote

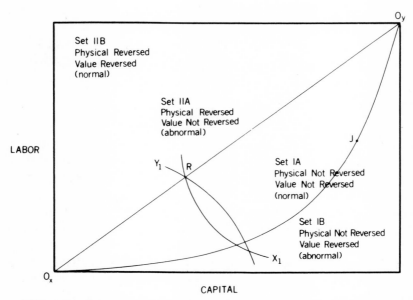

**FIG. 2.5.** Reversed and nonreversed relative physical and value factor intensities in the Edgeworth-Bowley box.

by sets I and II nonspecialized factor market equilibria for which
the physical factor intensities are not reversed or are reversed,
respectively. In Fig. 2.5, set I corresponds to nonspecialized points
below the diagonal and set II to nonspecialized points above the
diagonal.

We turn now to the effect of differentials on the relative value
factor intensities. Bhagwati and Srinivasan [27], Herberg and
Kemp [91], Jones [112], Lloyd [137], Magee [141], and
Mundlak [172] have all shown that factor price differentials can
reverse relative *value* factor intensities. We shall denote by sets A
and B nonspecialized factor market equilibria for which the original
value factor intensities are not reversed or are reversed, respectively.
For many production functions, it is possible for the value factor
intensities to reverse on both sides of the diagonal, so that we get
the four logical possibilities shown in Fig. 2.5.

For all production functions, all nonspecialized points between
the nondistorted efficiency locus $O_x J O_y$ and the diagonal $O_x R O_y$,
both inclusive, are members of set A [141]. Thus, the physical
and value factor intensities always correspond in the region between
the nondistorted contract curve and the diagonal in the Edgeworth-
Bowley box. The proof can be illustrated in Fig. 2.3 on p. 18. At
point A, $t = (r/w)_x /(r/w)_y > 1$, and VA in Eq. (2.20) can be rewritten

$$VA = \left(\frac{r}{w}\right)_y k_x \left(\frac{k_y}{k_x} - t\right) \qquad\qquad (2.21)$$

At all points below the diagonal in Fig. 2.3, $k_y /k_x$ is less than 1, by
assumption. But at all points above the nondistorted contract
curve $X_0 S Y_0$, t is greater than 1. Thus, $(k_y /k_x - t)$ is negative, VA
is negative between the nondistorted contract curve and the
diagonal, and PH is negative at all points below the diagonal.
Consequently, the physical and value factor intensities always
correspond in the region between the nondistorted contract curve
and the diagonal. This is an important result for the behavior of the
system to price and differential changes. We turn from this defini-
tional excursion to the economic effects of factor price differentials.

## 2.4  The Factor Market Effects

The theorems in this and in subsequent sections are developed using simple comparative statics analysis. For example, the effect on the economy of a change in t, the distortion parameter (holding P and k constant), is examined by taking the total derivatives of the endogenous variables with respect to t in ten of the eleven equations and solving. The process is the same for changes in P and k. In matrix terms, if $du_j/dt$ equals the change in variable $u_j$ with respect to a change in t, the solution can be written $[du_j/dt] = [f_{ij}]^{-1}[-f_{it}]$, where $f_{ij}$ is the partial derivative of equation i with respect to variable j and $-f_{it}$ is the partial derivative of equation i with respect to the parameter t. The notation and procedure are described by Samuelson [199, pp. 7-14]. The procedure used here was to drop one of the last five equations, calculate the matrix $[f_{ij}]$, and reduce it to the identity matrix using elementary row operations. Performing these row operations on a 10 × 10 identity matrix produced the desired matrix inverse $[f_{ij}]^{-1}$. An alternative solution is to observe clusters of equations which can be easily decomposed from the system and solved as subsystems; these solutions are then used in obtaining the solutions to subsequent clusters. For example, Eqs. (2.6) through (2.8) can be solved for $k_x$, $k_y$, and h, then Eqs. (2.4) and (2.5) for x and y, Eq. (2.10) for i, Eqs. (2.11) and (2.12) for $x^c$ and $y^c$, and Eqs. (2.16) and (2.17) for e and m.

Two cases are distinguished in this section: In case i, X is initially capital intensive (i.e., in the absence of distortion), and in case ii, X is originally labor intensive relative to Y. These two cases are illustrated in Fig. 2.6. Notice that the physical factor reversal value of t must be greater than 1 in case i and less than 1 in case ii.

The changes in the equilibrium capital-labor ratios in X and Y accompanying a change in the differential that X must pay for capital are

$$\frac{dk_x}{dt} = \frac{S_x}{k_y - tk_x}\left[\frac{g'Pk_x k_y f}{f'(f - k_x f')}\right] \tag{2.22}$$

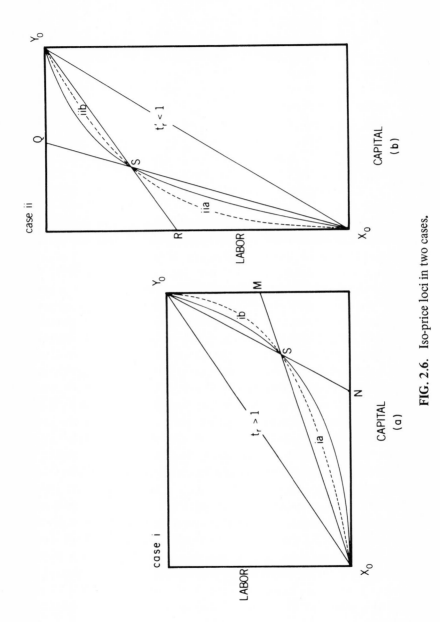

FIG. 2.6. Iso-price loci in two cases.

$$\frac{dk_y}{dt} = \frac{S_y}{k_y - tk_x}\left[\frac{k_x k_y g}{(g - k_y g')}\right] \qquad (2.23)$$

given

$$k_y - tk_x \neq 0$$

$$S_x \equiv \frac{f'(f - k_x f')}{k_x f f''}$$

$$S_y \equiv \frac{g'(g - k_y g')}{k_y g g''}$$

where $S_i$ ($< 0$) is the elasticity of factor substitution in industry i. Since the term in brackets on the right side of both equations is positive, the sign of the two equations depends on $k_y - tk_x$, i.e., the value factor intensities of the products [see Eq. (2.20)].

If $t = 1$, the term $k_y - tk_x$ is negative if industry X is originally capital intensive and positive if X is originally labor intentive. Furthermore, this same pattern of signs holds for all values of t between 1 and the value at which the physical factor intensities of the products reverse in both cases, as noted earlier (i.e., all points in the area between the nondistorted efficiency locus and the diagonal in the Edgeworth-Bowley box). In that area, an industry must be paying a differential for its intensive factor. Thus, we can generalize our earlier statement: If an industry pays a differential on the factor which is the intensive factor in the absence of distortion, a sufficient condition for the value and physical factor intensities to correspond is that the physical intensities have not reversed. If it pays a differential on its non-intensive factor, a necessary and sufficient condition for the two intensities to correspond is that the value intensity has not reversed.

From Eqs. (2.22) and (2.23), we have established the following. If the differential that X must pay for capital increases, then the capital-labor ratio increases in both industries if capital is the value-intensive factor in X and decreases if capital is not the value-intensive factor in X. Since there is a one-to-one relationship between the capital-labor ratios and relative factor prices because of the homogeneity assumption, the implication for relative factor prices is clear. If a factor in the first industry, for example, increases the differential that it receives there over the price of the same factor in the other industry, then, in the new equilibrium, that factor will be worse off in both industries if it is the value-intensive factor in the first industry and better off in both industries if it is not the value-intensive factor in the first industry. This has important implications for the distribution of income in distorted factor markets and for the exercise of market power by labor unions. If a labor union maintains a wage differential in the industry in which it is the value-intensive factor, then both union and non-union labor are worse off because of the union's shortsighted policy. Paradoxically, the unions would be wiser to organize in the industry in which labor is not the value-intensive factor.

The previous results are shown geometrically in Fig. 2.6. The solid line $X_0 SY_0$ is the traditional efficiency locus along which $t = 1$. Assume that the system starts from the nondistorted equilibrium point S in Fig. 2.6(a). An increase in t moves the factor market equilibrium to some point above the solid curved line $X_0 SY_0$ (since t now exceeds 1), below $X_0 SM$ [from Eq. (2.22), $k_x$ must rise], and to the left of $Y_0 SN$ [from Eq. (2.23), $k_y$ must rise]. Continuous increases in t move the system to distorted efficiency loci that are "farther" from the $t = 1$ locus, closer to the diagonal, and closer to $X_0$ because of the increases in $k_x$ and $k_y$, i.e., along the dashed line segment $X_0 S$ labeled ia in Fig. 2.6(a). The dashed lines ib, iia, and iib are generated in a similar manner in Figs. 2.6(a) and 2.6(b). Thus, if relative product prices are fixed (at some value that corresponds to a nondistorted factor market equilibrium point such as S), then the dashed line $X_0 SY_0$ represents a "distortion equilibrium locus," or what Marquez-Ruarte [148] calls an "iso-price locus," i.e., the locus of factor market equilibria for a fixed P and for alternative values of t. Of course, for sufficiently large and small values of t, the system will be completely specialized in one of the products.

Johnson and Mieszkowski [110] have discussed the possibility of physical factor intensity reversals whenever one of the industries pays a differential for its intensive factor. However, from Eqs. (2.22) and (2.23) and the previous discussion, we obtain another important result, namely, that physical factor intensity reversals can never be induced by changes in factor price differentials alone, short of complete specialization. The reason is that VA and PH always correspond between the diagonal and the nondistorted efficiency locus, and increases in a differential on the intensive factor in an industry *increase* rather than reduce the physical proportions of that factor used in production in both industries. This causes a widening rather than a narrowing of the observed relative physical intensities: continual increases in the differential with no change in relative product prices drives the system toward complete specialization in the industry not paying the differential.

Remember that relative product prices have been held constant throughout the process of changing the differential by our assumption that the country does not possess monopoly power in international trade. In order to highlight the importance of this assumption in obtaining the previous results, we start by differentiating the system with respect to P, with t and k fixed. The changes in the two capital-labor ratios are

$$\frac{dk_x}{dP} = \frac{S_x}{k_y - tk_x} \cdot \frac{tgk_x f}{f'(f - k_x f')} \tag{2.24}$$

$$\frac{dk_y}{dP} = \frac{S_y k_y g}{k_y - tk_x} \cdot \frac{(g - k_y g') + tg' k_x}{P_g'(g - k_y g')} \tag{2.25}$$

As before, the signs of Eqs. (2.24) and (2.25) depend on $k_y - tk_x$, and from the previous analysis we know that the signs are positive when X is value capital intensive and negative when X is labor intensive. Consequently, a change in relative product prices in the presence of distorted factor markets has the same qualitative effect on the capital-labor ratios in both industries when the value and physical factor intensities correspond as such a change in the absence of distortions.

One consequence of this result is that the Stolper-Samuelson theorem holds with one modification in distorted labor markets. As

Herberg et al. [94] have noted, the Stolper-Samuelson theorem holds for all interior points in the Edgeworth-Bowley box but the theorem must be stated in terms of the *value* rather than the *physical* factor intensities. Such a distinction was not necessary in the distortion-free case since the value and physical factor intensities always corresponded in that special case. Geometrically, an increase in P, the relative price of Y, for some fixed value of t (say, $t_b$ in Fig. 2.3 on p. 18) results in an increase in $k_x$ and $k_y$ and hence movement from a point such as B to B' along the iso-distortion locus $X_0 BY_0$.

We are now equipped analytically to explain the logic behind the response of factor markets to a change in a differential. In Fig. 2.7 we have combined an iso-distortion locus from Fig. 2.3 with an iso-price locus from Fig. 2.6 to illustrate the components of a change in the differential. Starting from a nondistorted equilibrium point S and increasing t to some value $t_a > 1$ while holding relative product prices constant yields two effects (see Johnson and Mieszkowski [110]). First, holding the output of X constant, there is a "substitution effect" in the industry paying the increased differential away from the factor receiving it, i.e., from S to A. Point A is on the iso-distortion curve $X_0 HGAY_0$ corresponding to $t_a$, the new value of t. Second, there is an "output effect," i.e., movement along $X_0 HGAY_0$ in the direction of $X_0$ since, as we shall observe shortly, the output of X must decline whenever X has to pay a higher differential. Notice that the *substitution* effect of the differential causes the capital-labor ratio to fall in X, as we would expect, while the *output* effect causes it to increase when X is capital intensive. The crucial question, which Johnson and Mieszkowski [110] and earlier studies did not answer clearly, is whether the output effect will be sufficient to outweigh the substitution effect and actually increase $k_x$ when product prices are fixed (geometrically, whether the output effect will place the new equilibrium above or below the old capital-labor ratio line $X_0 GM$). From Eq. (2.22) and the previous discussion, we know that the new equilibrium must be somewhere along the segment $X_0 HG$ rather than along GA. It will be at a point such as H, which defines a point on the iso-price locus $X_0 HSY_0$. Thus, the dominance of the output effect over the substitution effect explains the paradox of the increasing capital-labor ratio in X whenever X has to pay an increased differential for capital, its intensive factor. It should be noted that

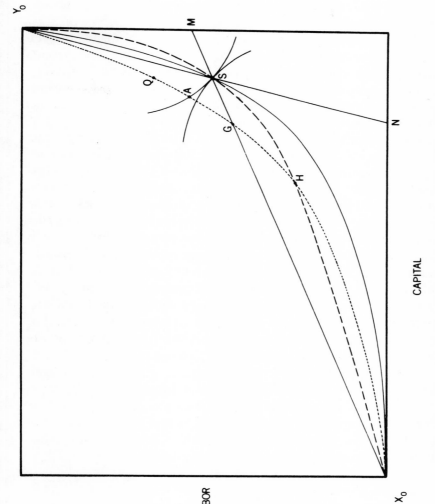

**FIG. 2.7.** The effects of introduction of a capital differential in industry X.

the output and substitution effects work against each other only when an industry must pay an increased differential for its intensive factor. Whenever the increased differential is on the nonintensive factor, the two effects will work together to move the capital-labor ratio in the direction which we would expect from the substitution effect.

If we relax the assumption that international demand is perfectly elastic (i.e., that relative product prices are fixed), we can add a third effect of a change in the differential, the "price effect." The substitution effect in Fig. 2.7 (S to A) plus the output effect (A to H) results in a decline in production of X and an increase in the production of Y. If this results in a lower relative price of Y, then $k_x$ may not increase if demand is sufficiently inelastic. From Eqs. (2.24) and (2.25), the capital-labor ratios must fall in X and Y as the relative price of Y falls, so that the price effect moves the system from H along the segment $HGAY_0$ in the direction of $Y_0$. If demand is sufficiently elastic, the new equilibrium will stay in the region HG so that the previous conclusions still hold. If, however, demand is not so elastic, then the new equilibrium point may fall in the region GA and the previous results are negated in that an increase in t now results in a decrease in $k_x$ when X is capital intensive. In this case, the relative return of capital *increases* in industry X and falls in Y. Thus, whether the price effect merely weakens the previous conclusions or changes them depends on product demand. For the remainder of this chapter, we shall maintain the original assumption that P is fixed.

## 2.5   The Output Effects

Before considering the effect of the differential t on the output of X and Y, we must first report the induced change in the proportion of labor allocated to the two industries (h to X and (1-h) to Y).

$$\frac{dh}{dt} = \frac{-k_x k_y}{(k_x - k_y)(k_y - tk_x)} \left[ \frac{hS_x g'Pf}{f'(f - k_x f')} + \frac{(1 - h)S_y g}{g - k_y g'} \right]$$

$$= \frac{[-h(dk_x/dt)] - [(1 - h)(dk_y/dt)]}{k_x - k_y} \tag{2.26}$$

Since $(k_x - k_y)$ and $(k_y - tk_x)$ represent the signs of the physical and value factor intensities, the change in h depends on whether the signs of these two terms correspond. Whenever a differential for capital *increases* in an industry, the proportion of the total labor supply employed there decreases if PH and VA have the same sign and increases if they do not. The change in the levels of output per laborer can now be expressed in terms of the changes in $k_x$, $k_y$, and h:

$$\frac{dx}{dt} = \frac{-k_x k_y f}{(k_x - k_y)(k_y - tk_x)} \left\{ \frac{S_x Pg'}{f(f - k_x f')} [hf - (k_x - k_y)] + \frac{S_y (1 - h)g}{g - k_y g'} \right\}$$

$$= f\frac{dh}{dt} + hf' \frac{dk_x}{dt}$$

$$(2.27)$$

$$\frac{dy}{dt} = \frac{gk_x k_y}{(k_x - k_y)(k_y - tk_x)} \left\{ \frac{S_x hPg'f}{f'(f - k_x f')} + (1 - h)\frac{S_y g}{g - k_y g'} + \frac{g'^2(k_x - k_y)}{g''gk_y} \right\}$$

$$= -g\frac{dh}{dt} + (1 - h)g' \frac{dk_y}{dt}$$

$$(2.28)$$

The changes in the outputs in Eqs. (2.27) and (2.28) are unambiguously determined only when both the proportion of labor and the amount of capital available for each laborer move in the same direction. When, however, one increases and the other decreases as in Eq. (2.27), when X is capital intensive, or Eq. (2.28), when Y is capital intensive, the signs are not obvious.

That which is ambiguous mathematically, however, is trivial geometrically. We shall use the powerful theorem that when exogenous changes cause the capital-labor ratios in both industries to move in the same direction, the changes in the outputs of both goods are unambiguously determined. This result holds for all interior points in the Edgeworth-Bowley box. It can be shown in Fig. 2.6 on p. 26: an increase in t always reduces X and increases Y.

Consider Fig. 2.6(a). An increase in the differential t implies that the capital-labor ratios in both the X and Y increase from Eqs. (2.22) and (2.23). This implies that the new factor market equilibrium must be below $X_0 SM$ and to the left of $Y_0 SN$, i.e., in the triangle $X_0 SN$. This triangle touches the intial X and Y isoquants at only one point. Thus, any movement away from that point as t increases implies that X must fall and Y must increase. The result holds for points both on and off the nondistorted contract curve.

The same argument applies to case ii, in which X is relatively labor intensive in the absence of distortion. An increase in the differential t results in a decrease in $k_x$ and $k_y$ from Eqs. (2.22) and (2.23). Thus, starting from point S, the new equilibrium must be to the left of $X_0$ SQ and below $Y_0$ SR. Again, X must decrease and Y must increase.

Notice that, in the two cases we have just considered, the physical and the value factor intensities corresponded. If, however, the value and the physical factor intensities do not correspond, so that the product is capital intensive according to one definition but labor intensive according to the other, then the same geometric arguments just presented can be used to show that an increase in the differential which the X industry must pay or a decrease in the relative product price of X will lead to an *increase* rather than a decrease in the output of X. Imagine, for example, that the physical factor intensities have been reversed while the value factor intensities have not, and that the product prices have been adjusted so that the system is in equilibrium at point D in Fig. 2.3 on p. 18. From Eqs. (2.22) and (2.23), an increase in t implies an increase in $k_x$ and $k_y$ when the value intensities have not been reversed. The new equilibrium must be to the right of a line extending from $X_0$ through D (not shown) and above a line extending from $Y_0$ through D. This implies a new equilibrium somewhere to the northeast of point D, meaning an *increase* in the production of X and a decrease in Y. From Eqs. (2.24) and (2.25), the same perverse results accompany changes in relative product prices. These results hold for all situations in which the physical and the value factor intensities do not correspond (cases IB and IIA in Fig. 2.5 on p. 23).

## 2.6 Rybczynski Growth and Technical Change

We turn to the behavior of the system when there is an exogenous increase in the economy's endowment of capital per man, k, in the present of a factor market distortion. We find that with P fixed internationally, the equilibrium capital-labor ratios are unaffected.

$$\frac{dk_x}{dk} = 0 \tag{2.29}$$

$$\frac{dk_y}{dk} = 0 \tag{2.30}$$

The changes in the output of X and Y per man are qualitatively identical to Rybczynski's [196]:

$$\frac{dx}{dk} = \frac{f}{k_x - k_y} > 0 \quad \text{when} \quad k_x > k_y \tag{2.31}$$

$$\frac{dy}{dk} = \frac{-g}{k_x - k_y} < 0 \quad \text{when} \quad k_x > k_y \tag{2.32}$$

Relative increases in the capital endowment cause the output of X to increase if X is physically factor intensive and to fall if it is not.

The effects of an exogenous increase in the supply of a factor are similar to those resulting from technical change in one of the industries. Specifically, consider Hicks-neutral technical change in the (linearly homogeneous) production of product X. This change is equivalent to a renumbering of the production isoquants for X in K-L space. If the technological change in the production of X is denoted by a change in the shift parameter a in the X production function, we obtain the following changes in the capital-labor ratios in the two industries:

$$\frac{dk_x}{da} = \frac{-Pt}{af''(k_y - tk_x)} \left[ \frac{g - k_y g'}{a} + g'k_y \right] \tag{2.33}$$

$$\frac{dk_y}{da} = \frac{-1}{g''(k_y - tk_x)} \left[ \frac{g - k_y g'}{a} + tk_x g' \right] \tag{2.34}$$

Thus, technical change in X increases the relative rates of return to capital in both industries if X is value-capital intensive and decreases them if X is value-labor intensive. Geometrically, Eqs. (2.33) and (2.34) can also be used to show that technical change in X increases X output when it is *value* capital intensive. As with no distortion, when X is capital intensive, neutral technical change in X results in the same output response as an increase in the relative supply of capital. This model and the Rybczynski model differ only in that the Hicks technical change model implies changes in the equilibrium capital-labor ratios while the Rybczynski model does not.

## 2.7  An Overview of Factor Market and Output Behavior with Distortions

The importance of the physical-value distinction for the entire system (not simply factor markets) is stressed by Jones [112]. His taxonomy is as follows. Physical factor proportions link changes in the real variables of the model, such as the community's outputs, and factor endowments. The value ranking given by distributive shares serves to link the "financial variables," i.e., the prices of outputs and rentals for the services of inputs. The relationship between changes in physical variables (e.g., outputs) and financial variables (e.g., output prices) depend crucially on whether physical and value rankings of factor proportions correspond. The use of the words "financial" and "real" does not imply the existence of any monetary assets in the model, but rather the distinction between relative price and share variables on the one hand and quantity variables on the other. The two definitions of factor intensity correspond (do not correspond) if PH and VA in Eqs. (2.19) and (2.20) on p. 22 have the same (opposite) sign.

For example, several recent papers [14, 27, 91, 94, 112, 137, 141, 172] arrive at the result that an increase in $P = P_y/P_x$ (with the differential held constant) increases the supply of Y if the physical and value intensities correspond and reduces Y if they do not. Consequently, the supply response of outputs to changes in P is *normal* if, and only if, neither the physical nor the value intensities are reversed (set IA in Fig. 2.5 on p. 23) or both are reversed (set IIB), and the response is *abnormal* if, and only if, relative factor intensities have reversed in the physical sense only (set IIA) or relative factor intensities have reversed in the value sense only (set IB). Thus, the supply of a product is positively related to relative product prices in the normal cases; supply is perfectly elastic with respect to prices whenever either the physical factor intensities of the products are identical or the value factor intensities of the products are identical [see Eqs. (2.27) and (2.28) on p. 33]; and supply is negatively related to prices in the abnormal cases.

The response of outputs to changes in the differential (with product prices constant) is similar [14, 94, 112, 141, 172]. An increase in a differential paid by an industry on either factor reduces output if the physical and value factor intensities correspond (the normal case) and increases output if they do not (the abnormal case).

## 2.8 Factor Price Differentials in the Samuelson-Johnson Factor Price Equalization Diagram

The factor market effects of a distortion can be incorporated into the Samuelson-Johnson diagram (Fig. 2.8). Assume initially that, in the absence of distortion, the equilibrium terms of trade are given by $(P_x/P_y)^e = 1/P$ so that relative factor prices at home and abroad equal $(r/w)^e$, and the capital-labor ratios in X and Y are $k_x^e$ and $k_y^e$. Note that Fig. 2.8 applies only to case i in Fig. 2.6(a) on p. 26, in which X is initially capital intensive, there are no reversals, and, by assumption, the country is capital abundant. Introduce any arbitrary value of t that does not cause complete specialization in either product. If $t > 1$, industry X pays a capital differential, and from Eqs. (2.22) and (2.23) we know that the dashed curves indicating the equilibrium factor price ratios for both industries lie below the nondistorted curve along which $t = 1$. The reason is that the increased differential raises the capital-labor ratios in both industries and hence lowers $(r/w)$ in both industries with product prices fixed. Conversely, if $t < 1$, both industry curves lie above the nondistorted curve. The curves in Fig. 2.8 relating $k_i$ to $r/w$ do not shift when t changes because of the homogeneity assumption. From Eqs. (2.24) and (2.25) we know that the distorted r/w curves are

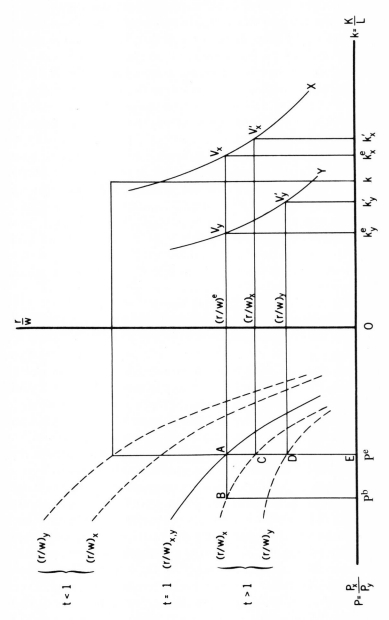

**FIG. 2.8.**  Differentials in the Samuelson-Johnson factor price equalization diagram.

positively sloped when X is value-capital intensive. In the two examples shown, the dashed curves are based on fixed values of t, as in Fig. 2.3 on p. 18. For different values of t, of course, both the location and distance between the two dashed lines will change. The differential t, which equals the ratio of X to Y's relative price of capital, equals CD/DE in the example in Fig. 2.8 in which $t > 1$.

Figure 2.8 also illustrates the variable product price case noted earlier. In the present context, assume that the foreign offer curve is less than perfectly elastic. If t increases from $t = 1$ at A to $t = CE/DE$, and $P_x/P_y$ increases from its original value $P^e$ because of reduced home production of X, then we still have $dk_x/dt > 0$ in case i as long as the new equilibrium product price ratio is not to the left of $P^b$. Figure 2.8 illustrates another property to be used subsequently, namely, that a differential breaks the one-to-one relationship between relative product prices and relative factor prices. (The one-to-one relationship is also broken in even another way: with differentials, multiple equilibria are possible.)

## 2.9 The Likelihood of Physical and Value Factor Intensity Reversals

In previous sections, we noted that reversals of physical and value factor intensities yield the four possible nonspecialized regions in the Edgeworth-Bowley box shown in Fig. 2.5 on p. 23. However, for certain production functions, some of these subsets may be null so that empirically, fewer than four nonspecialized regions will be observed. How large will the differential have to be to obtain the reversals discussed? This section comments on these issues.

For homothetic production functions, the ratio of the isoquant slopes along the diagonal in the Edgeworth-Bowley box yields the differential required to reverse the physical factor intensities (we shall see in the next chapter that the relative price of the good in the industry paying the differential must also be increased in order to cross the diagonal and move from set I to set II in Fig. 2.5).

In many situations, the differential required for physical reversal becomes smaller the higher the elasticities of factor substitution and the more similar the initial factor intensities of the products.

This statement can be demonstrated as follows. From Eq. (2.28) we can rewrite the change in output of one of the goods per capita, say good y, accompanying a change in the differential, t, as

$$\frac{dy}{dt} = \left[ \frac{-1}{(k_y - tk_x)(k_x - k_y)} \right] \left\{ -S_x \frac{ghg'Pk_xk_yf}{f'(f - k_xf')} \right.$$

$$\left. - S_y \frac{(1 - h)k_xk_yg}{(g - k_yg')} [g + g'(k_x - k_y)] \right\} \qquad (2.35)$$

Consider the case in which neither physical nor value intensity reversals have occurred. The derivative $dy/dt$ is clearly positive when X is relatively capital intensive since the first bracketed term and the term in braces are positive; it is also positive when X is relatively labor intensive, as noted in sec. 2.5. It appears that decreasing the differences in either the value $(k_y - tk_x)$ or the physical factor intensities $(k_x - k_y)$ or increasing the elasticity of substitution $S_x$ (absolutely) increases the absolute size of $dy/dt$, regardless of whether X or Y is capital intensive. The same holds if $S_y$ is increased when X is capital intensive; if X is labor intensive, the result still holds when $[g + g'(k_x - k_y)]$ is positive.

While it is difficult to generalize on the likelihood of *value* factor intensity reversals, the following statements can be made. (a) For Cobb-Douglas production functions, value factor intensity reversals are impossible since the distributive shares and hence the value factor intensities are invariant to changes in t and $P_x/P_y$ (see Herberg and Kemp [91]); thus, set B in Fig. 2.5 on p. 23 is null if $S_x = S_y = -1$. (b) If the physical factor intensities have not been reversed, value factor intensity reversals are possible only if an industry pays a differential on its nonintensive factor, which places the factor market equilibrium in the area on the side of the non-distorted efficiency locus opposite the diagonal in the Edgeworth-Bowley box [112, 141, 172]. (c) Herberg, et al. [94] proved that if t is held constant and $P_x/P_y$ varies, the value factor intensities never reverse if $S_x$ and $S_y$ are constant and equal, reverse only once if $S_x$ and $S_y$ are constant and different, and may reverse more than once in all other cases. They note that the reversal points, i.e., where $VA = 0$, need not be at a point which is consistent with incomplete specialization. They also show that for any given value of $k_y$ [along which $(r/w)_y$ is constant by the homogeneity assumption], the value intensities never reverse if $S_x = -1$, reverse once if $S_x$ is constant but unequal to $-1$, and may reverse more than once in all other cases. (d) Magee [144] has shown geometrically that, starting from any point in set IA in Fig. 2.5, a sufficient condition prohibiting value factor intensity reversals as t changes with $P_x/P_y$ constant is that $|S_x| \leqslant 1$ and $|S_y| \geqslant 1$.

Proposition (d) can be proved geometrically using the Samuelson-Johnson factor price equalization diagram in Fig. 2.8 on p. 38. Since the country does not possess monopoly power in trade, it faces a fixed world equilibrium product price ratio, $P^e$. The areas under the X and Y curves in the right-hand side of Fig. 2.8 equal the factor shares for capital relative to labor in each industry, $(rK/wL)_i$. The elasticities of factor substitution in the two industries, i.e., the percent change in $K/L$ for a given percent change in $r/w$, are equal to the elasticities of the X and Y curves.

Observe in Fig. 2.8 that, in the absence of distortion (t = 1), the physical and the value factor intensities of the two products must coincide. From Eq. (2.19), the differences in physical factor intensities at $(r/w)^e$ equal the linear *distances* from the origin of $k_x$ and $k_y$ along the k axis,

$$PH = Ok_y^e - Ok_x^e < 0 \tag{2.36}$$

while the difference in the value factor intensities from Eq. (2.20) are the differences in the *areas* under the X and Y curves, or

$$VA = \text{area } OV_y - \text{area } OV_x = \text{area } k_y^e V_x < 0 \tag{2.37}$$

As t increases to a value greater than 1, a separate $(r/w)_i$ curve must be drawn for each industry. When the value and the physical factor intensities correspond (do not correspond), the curves are positively (negatively) sloped. Whether capital increases or decreases its share of the value of output in each industry when t changes depends on the value factor intensities and on the elasticities of factor substitution, $S_i$. If $|S_i| > 1$, the share of capital in industry i and the area under the curve increases as the relative price of capital to i falls. If $|S_i| < 1$, the share of capital falls.

If industry Y, in which capital is the nonintensive factor, is forced to pay a differential for capital ($t < 1$), these results are simply reversed: capital is better (worse) off in both industries. Capital increases (decreases) its share of industry i's output if $|S_i| < 1$ ($|S_i| > 1$). If t decreases sufficiently, we get the case shown in Fig. 2.9 in which the value but not the physical factor intensities of the products have been reversed, since

$$VA_{t<1} = \text{area } OV'_y - \text{area } OV'_x > 0 \tag{2.38}$$

The dashed lines $(r/w)_i$ for $t < 1$ must be negatively sloped since the relationship $(r/w)_i = m_i(P_x/P_y)$ has the property $m'_i > 0$ without value reversal and $m'_i < 0$ with reversal.

In general, starting from any point in set IA in Fig. 2.5, reducing t moves points $V_x$ and $V_y$ up the X and Y curves in the right-hand side of Fig. 2.9. Geometrically, it is clear that VA will not change signs as t is decreased if the area under the X curve is constant or increases while the area under the Y curve is constant or decreases, i.e., $|S_x| \leqslant 1$ and $|S_y| \geqslant 1$. This completes the proof. Notice that the elasticities of substitution in this case do not need to be constant.

## 2.10 The Endogenous Differential

In this section we consider the case in which the differential itself is a variable and is adjusted by the factor with market power in response to changes in the system. We assume that capital introduces a differential t into industry X and that it changes the differential in response to changes in its relative price in X. Since the rental-wage ratio in X, $(r/w)_x$, is monotonically related to the capital-labor ratio in X, $k_x$, we can express this relationship as

$$t = t(k_x, c) \tag{2.39}$$

where c is a shift parameter.

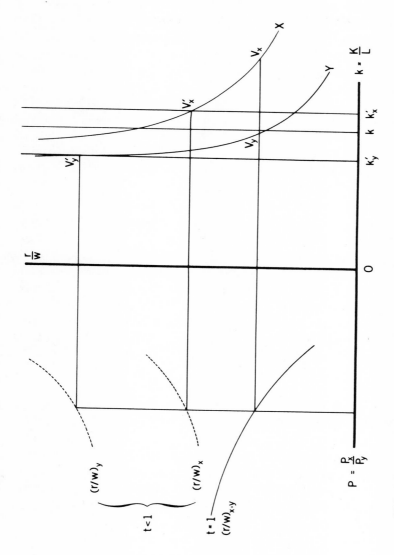

**FIG. 2.9.** A value factor intensity reversal in the Samuelson-Johnson factor price equalization diagram.

For convenience, start at a nondistorted equilibrium point, so that t = 1 initially. Since this implies a particular value of $k_x$, adjust the parameter c to a value $c_e$, which satisfies Eq. (2.40).

$$t(k_{xe}, c_e) = 1 \qquad (2.40)$$

The introduction of the differential into the model, reflecting newly acquired market power by capital in X, is accomplished by a shift in c. Thus, at every capital-labor in X, there is now a relatively higher rental paid for capital in X. The effect of this shift on the capital-labor ratios in X, Y and on the new level of t itself is shown in the following three equations:

$$\frac{dk_x}{dc} = \frac{\partial t}{\partial c} \frac{Pg'}{f''[1 - (tk_x/k_y)] - (\partial t/\partial k_x)Pg'} \qquad (2.41)$$

$$\frac{dk_y}{dc} = \frac{\partial t}{\partial c} \frac{S_y g f'(f - k_x f')}{S_x(g - k_y g')f\{f''[1 - (tk_x/k_y)] - (\partial t/\partial k_x)Pg'\}} \qquad (2.42)$$

$$\frac{dt}{dc} = \frac{\partial t}{\partial c}\left[1 + \frac{(\partial t/\partial k_x)Pg'}{f''[1 - (tk_x/k_y)] - (\partial t/\partial k_x)Pg'}\right] \qquad (2.43)$$

where

$S_x, S_y$ $(<0)$ = the elasticities of substitution

$\dfrac{\partial t}{\partial c} > 0$

$1 - \dfrac{tk_x}{k_y}$  $\begin{array}{l} < 0 \\ > 0 \end{array}$  $\begin{array}{l} \text{when X is value-capital intensive} \\ \text{when X is value-labor intensive} \end{array}$

$f', (f - k_x f')$  (in X) $\left.\right\}$ marginal products
$g', (g - k_y g')$  (in Y) $\left.\right\}$ of capital and labor

$\dfrac{\partial t}{\partial k_x}$ = the reaction parameter

First, we note that if the reaction parameter $\partial t/\partial k_x$ is equal to zero, then we get the results discussed in Sec. 2.3; namely, an increase in the differential on the intensive factor in an industry will lower its relative return in both industries while a differential on the nonintensive factor in an industry will raise its relative return in both industries.

Second, if capital, the value-intensive factor in X, reacts to declines in its relative price by shortsightedly raising the differential still further in an attempt to offset the decline ($\partial t/\partial k_x > 0$), its efforts are thwarted since the increased decline in the output of X reduces its relative price even more rapidly. This result applies to values of $\partial t/\partial k_x$ in the following range:

$$0 < \frac{\partial t}{\partial k_x} < w \qquad (2.44)$$

where

$$w = \frac{f''(k_y - tk_x)}{k_y Pg'}$$

When $\partial t/\partial k_x$ is larger than w, all of the previous results are reversed. In the new equilibrium, $k_x$, $k_y$, and t will have fallen, with the output of X increasing and that of Y declining. The system reacts wildly to the introduction of market power by the intensive factor when the reaction parameter $\partial t/\partial k_x$ is in the neighborhood of w. For values slightly above (below) w, a change in c induces a highly elastic supply response by producers.

While it may seem preposterous for the intensive factor in an industry to attempt to improve its market position by introducing a differential which lowers its real rate of return and then reacting to this decline by increasing the differential even further, this behavior is not without some empirical content. Such behavior results in elimination of the industry that pays the differential. Although a systematic investigation of the matter is not undertaken here, the unions and actors guilds in Hollywood and the railway labor unions come to mind as groups which have contributed to the decline in their industries. In both cases, the efforts of these groups to increase their return through market power hurt their industries and they reacted by pressing for even higher returns.

# Differentials, Prices, and the Transformation Curve

## 3.1 An Alternative Derivation of the Transformation Curve

This section outlines a geometric derivation of the production possibility curve and uses the technique to illustrate the "shrinkage effect" of factor price differentials. The derivation of the production possibility curve is simpler than the Savosnick [203] technique.

Assume, as before, that the two goods X and Y are produced using linearly homogeneous production functions utilizing capital and labor. Good X is relatively capital intensive in the absence of distortion, as shown in Fig. 3.1. Curve $O_x E_0 O_y$, the diagonal in Fig. 3.1, corresponds to the line $O_x' G_1' O_y$ in Fig. 3.1' (nonprimed points in Fig. 3.1 correspond to primed points in Fig. 3.1'). Since any units of measurement can be used for the outputs, choose the units of X so that the maximum output of X at $O_y'$ in Fig. 3.1' is directly above $O_y$ in Fig. 3.1. No restrictions are imposed on the units of Y so that $O_x'$ in Fig. 3.1' indicates the maximum amount of Y which is producible. Pick any arbitrary point $G_1$ on the diagonal in Fig. 3.1. Output of X equals $X_0$, and output of Y equals $Y_0$ (corresponding to point $G_1'$ with outputs $X_0'$ and $Y_0'$ in Fig. 3.1'). Hold Y output constant and move from $G_1$ to $E_0$ on the

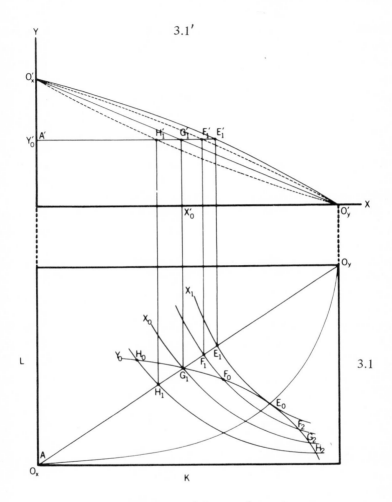

**FIG. 3.1.** Derivation of the transformation curve.

efficiency locus. Output of X increases from $X_0$ to $X_1$. Production isoquant $X_1$ cuts the diagonal at point $E_1$. Thus, holding Y output constant and moving to the efficiency locus yields an increase in X output corresponding to the ratio of $AE_1$ to $AG_1$ by the homogeneity assumption. Point $E_1'$ on the production possibility curve is constructed by setting $A'E_1/A'G_1$ equal to $AE_1/AG_1$. For example, if point $E_1$ is 20% farther from A than $G_1$, then point $E_1'$ on the production possibility curve is 20% to the right of $G_1'$. Movement from $G_1$ to $E_1$ in Fig. 3.1 is equivalent to multiplying both factor inputs by 1.20. By the homogeneity assumption, the new output level of X ($A'E_1'$) must also be 1.20 times the old output level ($A'G_1'$).

An alternative rule for locating $E_1'$ is to draw a vertical line from point $E_1$; the intersection of this line with $A'G_1$ extended to the right, point $E_1$ is the point on the production possibility curve corresponding to point $E_0$ on the efficiency locus. This concludes the derivation of the transformation curve.

We turn now to the effect of factor market distortions on the location of the production possibility curve. Profit maximization dictates that, in equilibrium, the slope of the production isoquant equal the ratio of rents to wages in each industry. Let $F_0$ be a factor market equilibrium point caused by a distortion. At $F_0$, the rental-wage ratio in the X industry exceeds that in the Y industry. At an unchanged level of Y output, the distortion causes the production possibility curve to shrink from $E_1'$ to $F_1'$. The ratio $O_x F_1/O_x E_1$ indicates the proportional shrinkage associated with the factor price differential at $F_0$ and the decrease in national income, measured at the original relative product prices (corresponding to point $E_1'$). As the factor price differential increases, Y output being held constant, X output decreases to $G_1'$, $H_1'$, etc. The reader is warned that the alternative production points considered here should not be construed as the results of an exercise in comparative statics. Increases in a differential do not imply decreases in one industry's output while the other's is constant in general equilibrium. Here we are simply locating points on distorted transformation loci.

Another result of this analysis is that points $F_1'$, $G_1'$, or $H_1'$ in Fig. 3.1' could have been generated by either higher relative prices for capital in industry X ($F_0$, $G_1$, or $H_0$ in Fig. 3.1) or higher relative prices for labor in X ($F_2$, $G_2$, or $H_2$). Consider all individual X and Y isoquants which intersect twice inside the Edgeworth-Bowley box. Each of these two intersections in factor space may be rather far apart (such as $G_1$ and $G_2$) and yet map into a single point in output space ($G_1'$).

We conclude this section with a simple rule for mapping any point in the Edgeworth-Bowley (E-B) box into output space. First, locate and connect with a straight line the two ends of the transformation curve as specified earlier. Second, pick any point in the E-B box, say $F_0$. There will be one X isoquant and one Y isoquant going through this point. Follow both isoquants to the diagonal in the E-B box. Draw a vertical line from the intersection of the Y isoquant with the diagonal (at $G_1$) until it hits the chord joining the ends of the transformation curve ($G_1'$); this fixes the output of Y ($X_0'G_1'$). Draw a horizontal line through this point ($A'E_1'$). (This line represents all possible output levels of X, given $X_0'G_1'$ of Y.) Return to the point in the E-B box where the X isoquant hits the diagonal ($F_1$). Extend a vertical line from this point until it intersects the horizontal line corresponding to the level of Y already determined (at $F_1'$). This intersection determines the level of X output ($A'F_1'$).

### 3.2 Shrinkage, Nontangency, and Multiple Differentials

In this section we shall examine jointly the problem of shrinkage of the transformation curve and its nontangency with the product price line in equilibrium. We have just noted how a single factor price differential may place the system below its optimum transformation curve in product space (the *shrinkage* effect). Point A in Figs. 3.2(a) and 3.2(b) indicates no distortion, while point D may indicate, for example, that X is paying a relatively higher price for capital than Y. Point D is on a transformation curve BDC in Fig. 3.2(b) which is inferior to the nondistorted curve BAC. Eckaus [53, p. 373] has called the outer curve the "technical transformation curve" and those inside of it "market transformation curves" since they are generated by factor market distortions. Fishlow and David [60] call them "outer" and "inner" transformation curves. We shall refer to them as "nondistorted" and "distorted" transformation curves. The element common to each curve is that the level of the factor price differential, t, is fixed along it. We noted in the previous section that points below the nondistorted (t = 1)

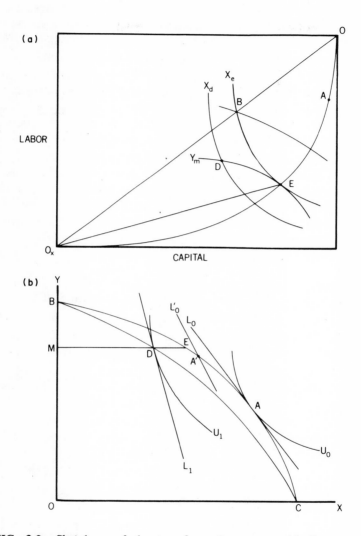

**FIG. 3.2.** Shrinkage of the transformation curve with factor market distortions.

transformation curve in output space may map into two points in the Edgeworth-Bowley box (one with $t > 1$ and the other with $t < 1$).

Factor price differentials can break the equivalence of the marginal technical rates of substitution between factors and the marginal rates of substitution and transformation between products. Consider the two-good, two-factor model discussed in Chap. 2. We can rewrite the first-order conditions for profit maximization as follows:

$$P_x X_\ell = w_x \tag{3.1}$$

$$P_y Y_\ell = w_y \tag{3.2}$$

$$P_x X_k = r_x \tag{3.3}$$

$$P_y Y_k = r_y \tag{3.4}$$

Where $X_j$ and $Y_j$ are the marginal products of the outputs with respect to the two inputs ($j = \ell, k$). A factor market distortion occurs whenever a differential exists such that $w_x \neq w_y$ or $r_x \neq r_y$. Following Hagen [75, pp. 507-508], we can take the total derivative of the production functions for both goods:

$$dY = Y_\ell \, dL_y + Y_k \, dK_y \tag{3.5}$$

$$dX = X_\ell \, dL_x + X_k \, dK_x \tag{3.6}$$

Next, take the ratio of Eq. (3.5) to Eq. (3.6) and substitute the values of the marginal products from Eq. (3.1) to Eq. (3.4):

$$\frac{dY}{dX} = \frac{(w_y/P_y) \, dL_y + (r_y/P_y) \, dK_y}{(w_x/P_x) \, dL_x + (r_x/P_x) \, dK_x} \tag{3.7}$$

Factor out $P_x$ and $P_y$ and note that, from the endowment constraint, $dL_y = -dL_x$ and $dK_y = -dK_x$. This yields

$$-\frac{dY}{dX} = \frac{P_x}{P_y} \left[ \frac{r_y \, dK_x + w_y \, dL_x}{r_x \, dK_x + w_x \, dL_x} \right] \tag{3.8}$$

The marginal rate of transformation (MRT) on the left-hand side of Eq. (3.8) differs from the marginal rate of substitution (MRS) represented by the product price ratio if the bracketed term in Eq. (3.8), which we shall call "the nontangency factor," differs from 1. With no distortions, $r_y = r_x$ and $w_y = w_x$ so that MRT = MRS.

### 3.2.1  The Single Differential

Consider the situation in which only one of the two factor markets is distorted. If industry X has to pay a higher price for capital $(r_x > r_y)$, the system moves above the efficiency locus to a point such as D in Fig. 3.2(a) so that

$$\frac{X_k}{X_\ell} = t\frac{Y_k}{Y_\ell} \tag{3.9}$$

where $t = (r_x/r_y) > 1$ is the ratio by which the slopes of the X isoquants exceed those of the Y isoquants; the marginal technical rates of factor substitution differ by $t - 1$. When $t > 1$, we can show from Eq. (3.8) that the nontangency factor is less than 1 so that MRS > MRT; i.e., the relative market price of X is greater than its opportunity cost because of the higher factor market costs of X induced by the differential:

$$-\frac{dY}{dX} = \frac{P_x}{P_y}\left[\frac{r_y\,dK_x + w_y\,dL_x}{tr_y\,dK_x + w_y\,dL_x}\right] \tag{3.10}$$

In Fig. 3.2(b), the slope of the price line $L_1 =$ MRS is greater than MRT, the latter being the slope of the distorted transformation curve BDC at D. When there is only one differential paid by one industry, the marginal equivalences are broken in both the *factor* and *product* markets. We get shrinkage of the transformation curve because of the former and nontangency of the price line with the distorted transformation curve at the equilibrium output because of the latter.

### 3.2.2 Identical Differentials on All Factors in the Same Industry

If industry X faces an identical differential t $(>1)$ for both factors, factor markets continue to operate along the nondistorted contract curve, since from Eqs. (3.1) through (3.4).

$$\frac{X_k}{X_\varrho} = \frac{tY_k}{tY_\varrho} \tag{3.11}$$

and the differentials cancel. Since we remain on the nondistorted contract curve in the Edgeworth-Bowley box, we remain on the nondistorted transformation curve BAC in output space in Fig. 3.2(b). The product markets are distorted, however, since substitution into Eq. (3.8) yields

$$-\frac{dY}{dX} = \frac{P_x}{P_y} \left[ \frac{r_y\, dK_x + w_y\, dL_x}{tr_y\, dK_x + tw_y\, dL_x} \right] \tag{3.12}$$

$$-\frac{dY}{dX} = \frac{P_x}{P_y} \cdot \frac{1}{t}$$

Thus, the MRT and the MRS differ by a factor of $1/t$. We have violated the marginal equivalences in product space so that price line $L_0'$ will intersect BAC from above at a point such as $A'$ in Fig. 3.2(b), with the nontangency factor less than 1. This case is similar to that of pure monopoly. The identical differential does *not* lead to *shrinkage* but it does lead to *nontangency*.

The implications of this case for the welfare effects of monopoly are rather interesting. If monopolies and oligopolies are confronted by strong labor unions which raise their wage above that for identical labor in other industries, then the higher returns to capital and to labor in such imperfectly competitive sectors result in no shrinkage of the transformation curve if both factors receive an identical differential. There is, however, a welfare loss due to the nonequivalence of the marginal rates of substitution and transformation.

### 3.2.3 Each Industry Pays a Differential
### for One of Its Factors

Myint [174] and others considered the possibility that in part of the postwar period the industrialized sector in less developed countries paid a differential for wages while the agricultural sector paid a differential for capital. If we let X be the sector producing and exporting agricultural products and Y the sector manufacturing import-competing products, then we have two differentials: $t = r_x/r_y > 1$ and $s = w_x/w_y < 1$. Assume X is capital intensive in the absence of distortion. To simplify, consider the case in which $s = 1/t$. The factor market equilibrium condition in this case is

$$\frac{X_k}{X_\ell} = \frac{t}{s}\frac{Y_k}{Y_\ell} = t^2\frac{Y_k}{Y_\ell} \tag{3.13}$$

This case results in an accentuated *shrinkage* of the transformation curve since the gap between the slopes of the production isoquants increases by a factor of $t^2$ as the differentials increase. In the normal situation, an increase in the differential which X must pay for capital encourages a reduction in its output, ceteris paribus, while an increase in Y's wage differential tends to reduce Y's output. This moves the equilibrium point in the E-B box more toward the diagonal than toward specialization in either X or Y. The two differentials have conflicting output effects. The changes in the capital-labor ratios in this double-differential case are

$$\frac{dk_x}{dt} = \frac{P[k_y g' - (g - k_y g')]}{tf''[(k_y/t) - tk_x]} \tag{3.14}$$

$$\frac{dk_y}{dt} = \frac{t^2 k_x g' - (g - k_y g')}{t^2 g''[(k_y/t) - tk_x]} \tag{3.15}$$

In the cases in which both outputs fall as a result of increases in t (and hence decreases in s), $k_x$ must fall and $k_y$ must rise. This is not obvious from the mathematics but it is clear geometrically (starting from E in Fig. 3.2(a), an increase in t moves the equilibrium northwest to a point above DE but below BE).

Although shrinkage to distorted transformation curves occurs more rapidly with double than with single differentials, the degree of nontangency between relative product prices and the equilibrium point on the distorted transformation curves is probably less pronounced with double differentials. The higher costs of capital in X are more or less offset by higher costs of labor in Y. The relationships among the marginal rate of transformation, ratio of product prices, and the nontangency factor are shown in Eq. (3.16).

$$-\frac{dY}{dX} = \frac{P_x}{P_y}\left[\frac{r_y\ dK_x + w_y\ dL_x}{tr_y\ dK_x + sw_y\ dL_x}\right] \tag{3.16}$$

When $t > 1$ and $s < 1$, it is not clear whether MRT is greater than, equal to, or less than MRS. The bracketed nontangency factor in Eq. (3.16) may equal 1 with an appropriate choice of s and t. In this case, there is severe shrinkage [see Eq. (3.13)] and yet there is no nontangency.

This case highlights the importance of distinguishing the two concepts: the *shrinkage* factor tells us how far below the nondistorted transformation curve the economy operates, and the *nontangency* factor indicates the extent to which observed supply prices do not reflect the economy's ability to transform one product into another. The present case of two differentials reducing the nontangency factor may have deceived some economists into thinking that two such differentials are less distortionary than one. For example, Meier [155, p. 393] made the following statement in his discussion of two differentials:

> The critical question, therefore, is whether manufacturing costs as a whole are overstated relatively (sic) to agricultural costs. This depends on the relative capital-labor ratios in the two sectors and the relative sizes of the wage and interest rate differentials between the two sectors. It is possible that the counter-balancing effects of the higher interest rate in agriculture and the higher capital-labor ratio in industry may more than offset the overvaluation of labor in industry.

Meier's statement applies only to the nontangency question. He was either unaware or simply failed to mention that another critical determinant of the welfare effects of differentials on an economy is the extent to which they have caused the system to shrink to distorted transformation loci.

## 3.3  The Shape of the Transformation Curve

We have noted the possibility of perverse supply response to relative product price changes. A related area which has drawn a considerable amount of theoretical investigation is the question of the shape of distorted transformation curves, i.e., their convexity. The problem has been examined by Bhagwati and Ramaswami [24], Bhagwati and Srinivasan [27], Fishlow and David [60], Herberg and Kemp [91], Johnson [105], Jones [112], and Lloyd [137], to name a few. While the question is of theoretical importance, it is, in my opinion, of little empirical importance. In Mundlak's [172, p. 531] words, "The examination of the convexity of the transformation curve is of little interest. What matters . . . is the relationships between [outputs] and [prices]." Independent investigations into the convexity question by Bhagwati and Srinivasan [27], Herberg and Kemp [91], and Lloyd [137] yielded the result that normal and perverse output responses to price changes are not necessarily related to the concacity or convexity (from below) of the distorted transformation curves. Thus, normal output response is possible along convex portions and perverse response is possible along concave portions of the transformation curve. This provides another reason for the practical unimportance of the convexity question.

However, many propositions have been derived linking the shape of the transformation curve to the factor market and production functions. We shall mention three:

1.  If a differential paid to the *intensive* factor in an industry (so measured in the absence of distortion) is large enough, it can cause the physical factor intensities to reverse. Before reversal, the transformation curve lies outside a chord joining its end points; at the reversal value, the

transformation curve coincides with the chord; after reversal, the transformation curve lies inside the chord (Johnson [105]).

2. In the Cobb-Douglas case, a differential paid by an industry on its *intensive* factor [yielding equilibria above the efficiency locus $O_x EO_y$ in Fig. 3.2(a) on p. 51] will be accompanied by a concave transformation curve with normal output response to price changes before physical reversal and a convex transformation curve with perverse output response after physical reversal (Johnson [105] and Herberg and Kemp [91]).

3. If, in the Cobb-Douglas case, a differential is paid by an industry on its *nonintensive* factor [yielding equilibria below the efficiency locus $O_x EO_y$ in Fig. 3.2(a)], then all output-price relationships are normal, regardless of the concavity or convexity of the transformation curve; in fact, the transformation curve may be uniformly convex or uniformly concave or partly concave and partly convex, but it cannot change its curvature more than twice (Herberg and Kemp [91]).

## 3.4  Differentials and Output Prices

We noted in Sec. 2.3 that the physical factor intensities could reverse. We defined set I (II) in Fig. 2.5 on p. 23 to be all nonspecialized factor market equilibria for which the physical factor intensities were not reversed (reversed). With homogeneous production functions, it is clear that all values of the differential t in set II exceed the values of t in set I [94, 105, 110, 141, 172]. What about relative product prices in sets I and II? Magee [140, 141] showed that it is impossible to move from set I to set II by merely changing the differential since (a) reversal can occur only with an industry paying a differential on its intensive factor, and (b) while increasing the differential moves the system closer to set II in Fig. 2.5, complete specialization must come first since both factor ratios increase (i.e., the ratios of the physically intense factor in the industry paying the differential to the other factor; when X is capital intensive, $k_x$ and $k_y$ both increase when t increases—see Sec. 2.4).

Herberg et al. [94] extended this, proving that the set of relative product prices giving nonspecialized equilibria below the diagonal in the Edgeworth-Bowley box and the set of relative product prices giving equilibria above the diagonal are mutually exclusive. In terms of the model developed in Chap. 2, all of the values of t and $P_x/P_y (= 1/P)$ in set II exceed the values of t and $P_x/P_y$ in set I in Fig. 2.5. In order to cross the diagonal and remain nonspecialized, *both* the differential and relative product prices must change.

The proposition that the relative price of X increases as non-specialized factor market equilibrium points move across the diagonal in the Edgeworth-Bowley box can be illustrated in Fig. 3.3. Consider movement across the diagonal in the box along any X isoquant, say $X_0$, starting from point $E_0$. Increase the differential paid by the X industry for capital from $t_0$ to $t_1$ ($> 1$). We know from Eq. (2.22) on p. 25 that the new equilibrium must be at a higher capital-labor ratio in industry X. Thus, the new equilibrium will be below the straight line $O_x E_0$, such as point $A_1$. Point $A_1$ is located on an iso-distortion locus corresponding to differential $t_1$. From Eqs. (2.24) and (2.25) we know that, in order for the factor market equilibrium to move along this locus from $A_1$ to $E_1$, a point on the original X isoquant, the relative price of X must increase. Thus, in moving from $E_0$ to $E_1$, both the differential paid by X and the relative price of X must increase. As the differential increases from $t_1$ to $t_2$ with prices constant, the equilibrium moves from $E_1$ to $A_2$. With the differential fixed, the relative price of X must increase (to get back to $X_0$) until the equilibrium moves to point $E_2$. Clearly, both t and $P_x/P_y$ must increase as the factor market equilibria move from $E_0$ to $E_3$.

At $E_3$ in Fig. 3.3, the differential has reached the unique value at which the physical factor intensities reverse, $t_r$. Let us now analyze what happens after the physical factor intensities have reversed. If we are above the diagonal but still sufficiently close to it, the value factor intensities [represented by the term $(k_y - tk_x)$ in Eqs. (2.22) through (2.25)] will not have reversed. Thus, the physical and the value factor intensities do not correspond and we are in a region of perverse output response (set IIA in Fig. 2.5). Starting from $E_4$, increase the differential t. From Eqs. (2.22) and (2.23), we know that the new equilibrium must be to the right of the extended line $O_x E_4$ and above the line $O_y E_4$, such as $A_5$.

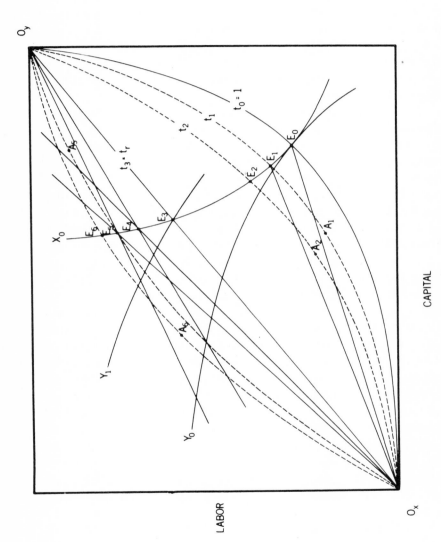

**FIG. 3.3.** Physical factor intensity reversal with price and distortion changes.

Point $A_5$ is on the iso-distortion locus $O_x E_5 A_5 O_y$. In order to move from $A_5$ back to the original level of output $X_0$ at $E_5$, we must increase rather than decrease the relative price of X (because of the perverse relationship between outputs and prices) so that both capital-labor ratios will fall [see Eqs. (2.24) and (2.25)]. Thus, movements above and away from the diagonal along isoquant $X_0$ in set IIA imply continuous increases in the relative price of X.

Assume that the system moves into a region in which the value factor intensities have also reversed (corresponding to set IIB in Fig. 2.5). Do increases in t in this region also imply increases in the relative price of X? Assume that, at $E_5$ in Fig. 3.3, the value factor intensities of the product have reversed. As the differential t is increased, the capital-labor ratios in both industries fall. This implies that the new equilibrium point must be above the straight line $O_x E_5$ and below the extended line $O_y E_5$, at a point such as $A_6$. But, from Eqs. (2.24) and (2.25), we know that in order to move from $A_6$ to $E_6$, the relative price of X must increase. (In this region, where both the physical and the value factor intensities have reversed, the output responses to differential and price changes is normal.) A similar demonstration can be made for points in set IB in Fig. 2.5: moving southeast along $X_0$ and away from the diagonal results in reductions in t and decreases in $P_x/P_y$.

If the relative price of X is always increasing as we cross the diagonal, we need only demonstrate that the $P_x/P_y$ corresponding to equilibrium along the diagonal is unique in order to establish the mutual exclusivity of relative product prices in sets I and II. We know from the homogeneity postulate that $dY/dX$ is constant as we move along the diagonal from $O_x$ in Fig. 3.3 to $O_y$. We know from Fig. 3.1' that the transformation curve is a chord joining the two end points, $O_x'$ and $O_y'$. We must now establish the constancy along $O_x O_y$ of the nontangency factor. Rewriting Eq. (3.8), we have

$$-\frac{dY}{dX} = \frac{P_x}{P_y}\left[\frac{r_y\, dK_x + w_y\, dL_x}{r_x\, dK_x + w_x\, dL_x}\right] \tag{3.17}$$

Along the diagonal, $dK_x/dL_x = k$, the country's factor endowment ratio, so that Eq. (3.17) can be written

$$-\frac{dY}{dX} = \frac{P_x}{P_y}\left[\frac{r_y k + w_y}{r_x k + w_x}\right] \tag{3.18}$$

Since $w_y = w_x$ with the single factor price differential, Eq. (3.18) can be rewritten

$$-\frac{dY}{dX} = \frac{P_x}{P_y}\left[\frac{(r/w)_y k + 1}{(r/w)_x k + 1}\right] \tag{3.19}$$

Since $(r/w)_x$ and $(r/w)_y$ equal the slopes of the X and Y isoquants along the diagonal, which are constant by the homogeneity assumption, the bracketed term in Eq. (3.19), i.e., the nontangency factor, is constant along the diagonal in the Edgeworth-Bowley box. Since $dY/dX$ is constant [and, from the discussion preceding Eq. (2.4), equal to $-g(k)/f(k)$] Eq. (3.19) can be used to solve for the equilibrium product price ratio along the diagonal (the actual equilibrium point along the straight line transformation curve is indeterminate):

$$\begin{aligned}\left(\frac{P_x}{P_y}\right)_r &= \frac{g}{f}\left[\frac{(r/w)_y k + 1}{(r/w)_x k + 1}\right] \\ &= \frac{g(k)}{f(k)}\left\{\frac{kf'(k)/[f(k) - kf'(k)] + 1}{kg'(k)/[g(k) - kg'(k)] + 1}\right\}\end{aligned} \tag{3.20}$$

where $(P_x/P_y)_r$ is the price ratio at which the physical factor intensities of the products reverse. As shown in Eq. (3.20), it is unique, given the country's factor endowment and the production functions for the two goods.

Thus, we have established that (a) upward movement along any fixed X isoquant implies continuous increases in the differential and in the relative price of X if such a point is to be an equilibrium point, and (b) the unique value of the relative product price ratios corresponding to equilibrium along the diagonal in the E-B box forms the upper bound on all nonspecialized equilibrium product prices below the diagonal and the lower bound on all relative product prices above the diagonal. The implications of these mutually exclusive sets of product prices are interesting and important for several theoretical points to be developed later. They imply, for example, that any relative price ratio giving non-specialization along a nondistorted transformation curve cannot yield a nonspecialized factor market equilibrium if a differential, t, is introduced which exceeds the reversal value, $t_r$. A more general statement is that the equilibrium of an economy can never move across the diagonal in the Edgeworth-Bowley box by a change in the differential alone with nonspecialization occurring on *both* sides of the diagonal.

# International Trade, Factor Movements, and Welfare with Differentials

## 4.1 Trade Reversals and the Leontief Paradox

We turn to the effects of differentials on the pattern and level of trade in a small country. This analysis has some interesting implications for empirical studies which have attempted to test the Heckscher-Ohlin theorem, since factor market distortions can reverse both factor intensities and the pattern of trade.

The result that the trade pattern can be reversed by factor market distortions is not a new idea. It has been known that such distortions can disrupt theories of comparative advantage since at least 1874, when Cairnes [41] elaborated his theory of non-competing groups. But until Magee's study [140], no studies of trade and distortions had succeeded in explaining how capital-labor ratios behaved as differentials changed; thus, they could make little headway in exploring reversals of the Heckscher-Ohlin theorem fully because of the prominent role that the factor marked played in that theorem.

We start the analysis by employing the model used in Chap. 2: variables e and m are exports and imports per laborer in the country. As before, we assume that industry X pays a differential for capital, so that $t = r_x/r_y \neq 1$. The changes in exports and imports per capita accompanying a change in t are

$$\frac{de}{dt} = \left(1 - \frac{\partial x^c}{\partial i}\right)\frac{dx}{dt} - \frac{\partial x^c}{\partial i}\frac{dy}{dt} \qquad\qquad (4.1)$$

$$\frac{dm}{dt} = \frac{1}{P}\frac{de}{dt} \qquad\qquad (4.2)$$

where superscript c denotes consumption and i is national income per laborer. Assume that in the absence of distortion (t = 1) the country conforms to the Heckscher-Ohlin theorem in exporting product X, which uses relatively intensely the country's abundant factor, and that domestic factor prices are equal to those abroad. Let case i in Fig. 2.6(a) on p. 26 show the case in which X is capital intensive and the country is capital abundant, and let case ii in 2.6(b) show the opposite possibility. In both cases, point S represents the initial nondistorted free-trade equilibrium. Assume initially that no factor intensity reversals have occurred. Equations (4.1) and (4.2) indicate that, if X is neither a luxury nor an inferior good in consumption, an increase in a differential paid by the import-competing industry on either factor increases both exports and imports as production in the export industry declines and production in the import-competing industry expands. In Fig. 2.6, the export industry X pays a differential for capital in cases ia and iia (t > 1), while the import-competing industry Y pays a differential for capital in cases ib and iib (t < 1).

It is clear that a reversal of the pattern of trade is possible only when the export industry pays a differential (t > 1). In this case, we shall denote by $t_{tr}$, as before, value of the differential at which the pattern of trade reverses (at that point, e = m = 0). Factor price differentials thus have a direct impact on the importance of trade in the national economy (the share of trade in GNP). The importance of trade increases as the differential t moves away in either direction from the trade reversal value $t_{tr}$. For all values of the differential short of $t_{tr}$, the country continues to export the product that the Heckscher-Ohlin theorem predicts. For all values of the differential beyond $t_{tr}$, however, the pattern of trade is reversed and the country exports the product that uses relatively intensely the country's *scarce* factor. In this case, we have used the physical definition of the country's relative factor abundance in applying the Heckscher-Ohlin theorem, i.e., compared the country's relative physical factor abundance in applying the Heckscher-Ohlin theorem. But even if we use the second means of defining relative factor abundance, the pretrade factor price ratios (see Bhagwati [20, p. 19]), the Heckscher-Ohlin theorem can still fail to predict correctly the pattern of trade, since we illustrated in Fig. 2.8 on p. 38 that the one-to-one relationship between product prices and factor prices is broken by factor price differentials. Notice there that even if the country in question is relatively capital abundant, if the import-competing industry Y pays a capital differential, the resulting increases in the relative price of capital to both industries may make the country appear capital scarce relative to the rest of the world. Bhagwati and Srinivasan [27] have cited another interesting pathology: reversal of the value factor intensities makes multiple equilibria possible so that even if two countries have the same production possibilities, the same differential, and the same tastes with homotheticity, trade is possible between them if one country has the first equilibrium and the other country the second of, say, two equilibria.

The reversal of the trade pattern can be illustrated in output space in Fig. 4.1. Without factor distortions, production in free-trade equilibrium occurs along the transformation curve UVU' at V, domestic consumption occurs at T' (the intersection of the linear income-consumption curve ICC and the international price line $L_1$), and exports of good X equal Z'Z. The ICC curve shown represents a locus of tangencies of domestic (homothetic) community indifference curves and relative price lines whose slopes equal the slope of $L_1$. If the differential paid by X increases sufficiently, the new production point may move to H on a distorted transformation curve and consumption to T so that the trade pattern is reversed and the country now imports W'W of X. The slope of $L_2$, the international terms of trade, equals the slope of $L_1$ by the small-country assumption. In terms of Fig. 4.1, *trade reversal occurs at the value of the differential at which the production point crosses the Engel's curve,* ICC.

We have noted that, starting from any nondistorted equilibrium

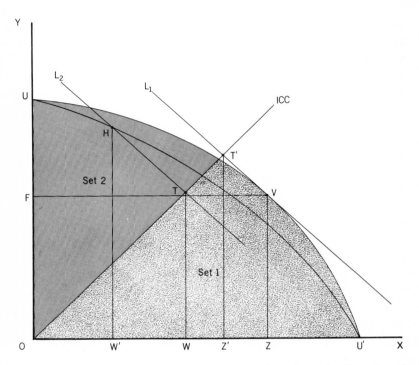

**FIG. 4.1.** Determination of the pattern of trade with distortion determined production points: in set 1(2), X is exported (imported).

point, introduction of a factor price differential in a small country on either factor in the export sector reduces trade and can lead to the trade pattern reversal. Introduction of a differential on either factor in the import-competing industry causes the Heckscher-Ohlin theorem to be spuriously strengthened as resources which are released from the import-competing sector and absorbed by the export sector increase both exports and imports (remember that the discussion to this point has not admitted factor intensity reversals).

We shall denote by sets 1 and 2 nonspecialized factor market equilibria for which the pattern of trade does or does not correspond to the pattern which would exist in the absence of distortion. Assume that the country is relatively capital abundant and good X is relatively capital intensive without distortion. Thus, good X is always exported in set 1 and good Y in set 2. Assume, for simplicity, that the country has homothetic community indifference curves so that the ICC curve shown in Fig. 4.1 is a straight line. Since the country faces a fixed international terms of trade, as we have assumed, the only information required to determine the pattern of trade is the ratio of the production of X to Y. If the home country production ratio X/Y exceeds the free-trade consumption ratio $(X/Y)^c$, good X is exported, while the converse holds if X/Y is less than $(X/Y)^c$. In Fig. 4.1, $(X/Y)^c$ equals the inverse of the slope of the linear ICC curve; notice that if factor price differentials cause the production point to fall anywhere below ICC, good X is exported (set 1) while all production points above the ICC imply that good X is imported (set 2).

The reason for imposing homotheticity on consumer demand is that it allows us to compare all possible production points with a single scalar, $(X/Y)^c$, in order to determine the pattern of trade. Next, we construct a locus of points in the Edgeworth-Bowley box at which the ratio of production of X to Y equals $(X/Y)^c$. In Fig. 4.2, this locus is the line GH. At all points to the right of GH, X/Y in production exceeds $(X/Y)^c$ so that X is exported (set 1) while, at all points to the left of GH, Y is exported (set 2).

Before we can discuss whether the country conforms to the Heckscher-Ohlin theorem or whether it yields "Leontief-type results," we must discuss the two possible definitions of factor intensity which could be used in the test. As in Chap. 2, let PH represent the physical definition of relative factor intensity, i.e., the difference in the capital-labor ratios in the two industries.

$$PH = k_y - k_x \qquad (4.3)$$

Similarly, let VA represent the value definition of relative factor intensity, i.e., the difference in the shares of capital relative to labor in the two industries.

$$VA = \frac{r_y K_y}{w_y L_y} - \frac{r_x K_x}{w_x L_x} \qquad (4.4)$$

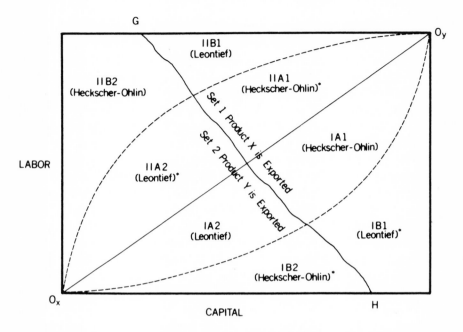

**FIG. 4.2.** Heckscher-Ohlin and Leontief-Type regions in the Edgeworth-Bowley box.

In the absence of distortion (when t = 1), remember that both PH and VA are always negative when X is capital intensive, so that along the nondistorted contract curve in the Edgeworth-Bowley box, the physical factor intensities and the value factor intensities of the products correspond. Finally, we shall define the measure of factor intensity which Leontief [129-132] and most researchers have used in testing the Heckscher-Ohlin theorem, LE, which is the relative value of capital per man (or man-year) in the export and import-competing sectors.

$$LE = \frac{r_y K_y}{L_y} - \frac{r_x K_x}{L_x} \qquad (4.5)$$

Obviously, LE and VA have the same sign, in the absence of wage distortions, so that Leontief's measure corresponds to the definition of factor intensities in the value sense. Because of this correspondence between LE and VA, we shall use only the PH and VA definitions of factor intensities in the subsequent analysis.

Given the possible cases shown in Fig. 2.5 on p. 23 and the previous discussion, we are now equipped with a taxonomy of the theoretical possibilities generated by factor price differentials: the physical factor intensities may or may not be reversed (sets II and I); the value factor intensities may or may not be reversed (sets B and A); and the pattern of trade may or may not be reversed (sets 2 and 1). Thus, admitting the entire Edgeworth-Bowley box to scrutiny yields the eight regions shown in Fig. 4.2.

We turn to the question of the verifiability of the Heckscher-Ohlin theorem in the presence of factor market distortions. Assume that the country is abundant relative to the rest of the world in its endowment of physical capital and that we wish to test whether its exports are capital intensive (confirming the applicability of the Heckscher-Ohlin theorem) or labor intensive (rejecting the theorem). The results of such tests depend on how the factor intensities of exportables and import-competing production are defined.

First, let us proceed, as Leontief, and examine the sign of LE in Eq. (4.5), which is equivalent to measuring factor intensities in the *value* sense. Clearly, we can get Leontief-type results in four of the eight regions in Fig. 4.2; the only requirement is that the good exported be labor intensive in the value sense. This occurs when either the pattern of trade is reversed or the value factor intensities are reversed but not both, i.e., in cases IA2, IIA2, IB1, and IIB1. On the other hand, if neither trade nor the value intensities are reversed or if both are reversed, the Heckscher-Ohlin theorem holds in the remaining four regions: cases IA1, IIA1, IB2, and IIB2. Region IIB2 is interesting since the physical factor intensities, the value factor intensities, and the pattern of trade are all reversed and yet exports of Y are observed to be capital intensive, apparently confirming the applicability of the Heckscher-Ohlin theorem.

Let us now perform the same exercise, but test the relative factor intensity of exports using the *physical* measure given in

Eq. (4.3). As before, there are the eight logical possibilities shown in Fig. 4.2. But, since the value and the physical factor intensities can differ with differentials, two regions in Fig. 4.2 which were formerly classified as Heckscher-Ohlin now become Leontief (IB2 and IIA1), while two Leontief regions become Heckscher-Ohlin (IB1 and IIA2). These four regions are denoted by an asterisk. The results in the other four regions are invariant to the definition of factor intensity since the physical and value factor intensities correspond in those regions.

These results are equally devastating for studies which compare the factor intensities of exports relative to imports, assume that the Heckscher-Ohlin theorem applies, and then infer the relative factor abundance of the country. In the presence of the distortions we have discussed, in four out of the eight cases the country's factor abundance will be predicted incorrectly. Again, in half of the cases, the results depend on which definition of factor intensity is used.

Reversals of physical and value factor intensities and trade yield a maximum of eight possible nonspecialized regions in the Edgeworth-Bowley box. Remember, however, that for certain production functions, some of these subsets may be null so that in practice fewer than eight nonspecialized regions may be observable. Also, large values of the differential may be required to obtain the reversals discussed (see Sec. 2.9).

One caveat must be placed on these results. In Sec. 3.4 we observed that the set of relative supply prices giving nonspecialized equilibria below the diagonal in the Edgeworth-Bowley box and the set of prices giving equilibrium above the diagonal are mutually exclusive. All of the values of t and $P_x/P_y$ in set II exceed the values of t and $P_x/P_y$ in set I in Fig. 4.2. Thus, in this chapter, in addition to an increased differential, we must introduce some distortion in product markets which allows $P_x/P_y$ facing domestic producers to exceed the world market price if we are to move from set I to set II and remain nonspecialized. For simplicity, assume that this is either a production subsidy to industry X or a production tax on industry Y. Either of these distortions permits domestic consumption to continue to occur at world market prices.

## 4.2 Trade and Factor Movements

Consider first the effect on trade of an exogenous inflow of physical capital into a country with distorted factor markets. The effect of this inflow is to increase the country's endowment of capital per man. Differentiating the system with respect to k and solving, we obtain the effects on trade:

$$\frac{de}{dk} = \frac{dx}{dk} - \frac{dx^c}{dk} = \frac{f(1 - \partial x^c/\partial i) + (\partial x^c/\partial i)Pg}{k_x - k_y} \tag{4.6}$$

$$\frac{dm}{dk} = \frac{1}{P}\frac{de}{dk} \tag{4.7}$$

Thus, if good X is neither a luxury nor inferior, an increase in a country's endowment of capital per man algebraically increases exports when they are physically capital intensive and decreases them when they are not. Imports move in the same direction as exports.

Consider second the implications of differentials for factor prices, assuming that export and import-competing industries are so designated in the absence of distortions and that *no reversals* have occurred. If the export industry pays a differential, the price of the country's physically abundant factor in both industries will be below the price in nondistorted factor markets abroad with free trade. If the country is capital abundant and X is the capital-intensive industry paying the capital differential, then this case is shown in Fig. 2.8 on p. 38 in which t > 1. (The nondistorted curve along which t = 1 represents nondistorted foreign factor prices.)

If the import-competing industry pays the capital differential, the price of the country's physically abundant factor in both industries will be above the price in nondistorted factor markets abroad with free trade (the case in which t < 1 in Fig. 2.8). In this case, we get the paradoxical result that factors will want to move from countries where they are scarce to countries where they are already abundant.

Consider now the effect of differentials on international factor movements. Assume for a moment that capital becomes mobile internationally, while labor does not. From Eqs. (2.22), (2.23), and (2.29) through (2.32), we can establish the following. (The numbers in parentheses refer to the relevant cases in Fig. 2.6 on p. 26). If capital is the intensive factor in the industry paying the differential, then capital will leave the country to obtain higher rates of return abroad (ia and iib), while if it is the nonintensive factor, capital will flow into the country for the higher domestic rate of return (ib and iia). With fixed international product prices (because of the small-country assumption), these capital movements will not affect $k_x$, $k_y$ and hence domestic factor prices. If capital is going abroad, the country will approach complete specialization in the labor-intensive product (Y in ia and X in iib). If capital is flowing in, the country will move toward specialization in the capital-intensive product (X in ib and Y in iia).

Since these capital movements affect the country's factor endowments, they will either strengthen or weaken (and possibly reverse) what would have been the original pattern of trade. If the *import-competing* industry pays the capital differential, the original trade pattern will be strengthened as exports and imports increase and factor endowments become more dissimilar. To illustrate this, consider the two possibilities. When exports are initially *capital* intensive, r/w in both domestic industries increases as t falls (case ib). This attracts foreign capital and expands both exports and imports as the capital-intensive export sector expands and the import-competing sector is eliminated. When exportables are initially *labor* intensive, r/w falls at home in both industries as t decreases (case iib). This causes capital to leave the country, which again expands exports and imports as the capital-intensive, import-competing industry contracts and the export industry expands. If the *export* industry pays the capital differential, exports and imports will fall and the original trade pattern can reverse.

Notice that these results accentuate those obtained in Sec. 4.1. There, introduction of a capital differential expands trade if it is paid by the import-competing sector and contracts trade if it is paid by the export sector. Starting from this new distorted equilibrium point, introduction of international capital mobility generates physical capital movements which expand trade even further if the differential is paid by the import-competing industry or reduce trade if the differential is paid by the export sector. In the latter case, the reduction in trade continues to the trade reversal point and then trade expands as complete specialization in production occurs.

Finally, if tariffs are present and if distorted domestic factor markets cause capital to be less mobile between domestic industries than internationally, we can get international capital cross flows, e.g., domestic capital emigrating from the X industry and foreign capital entering the Y industry. This possibility is shown in Fig. 4.3. Assume that the world price is $(P_x/P_y)_E = OF$ and that factor markets abroad are not distorted so that foreign factor prices equal $(r/w)_E = FA$. Assume that industry Y pays a capital differential (t $<1$) and that it trys to offset this disadvantage by having the government impose an ad valorem tariff on imports of Y equal to, say, $(OF/OG) - 1$, so that the domestic price of X relative to Y equals OG. As a result, r/w in industry X (GJ) is less than r/w abroad (GI), causing capital to emigrate from X. If foreign capital is able to circumvent whatever barriers to entry that industry Y enforces against home capital, then it will enter the Y industry since r/w in Y at home (GH) exceeds the foreign ratio (GI).

## 4.3  Trade and Welfare

The welfare consequences of factor price differentials in both one- and two-factor models have elicited considerable interest. Manoilesco [146] started the debate in 1931 with his observation that Eastern European countries were being hurt by trade with Western Europe because free trade was forcing them to specialize in slow-growth and low-productivity agricultural products while Western Europe benefited from specialization in manufactured products, where productivity was higher. The differentials in the marginal productivities in the two sectors convinced him that protection of the manufacturing industries in less developed countries would be superior to free trade. This theme was

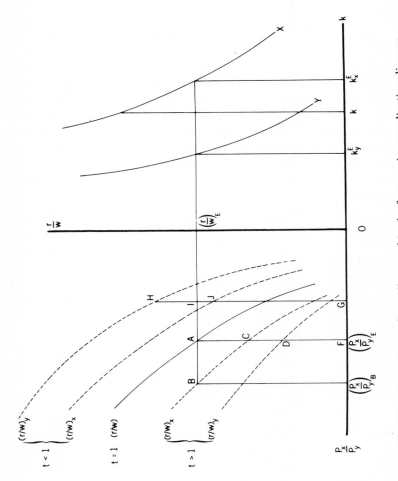

**FIG. 4.3.** Capital cross-flows illustrated in the factor price equalization diagram.

formalized for both one- and two-factor models by Hagen [75].
At least three propositions can be stated on this issue.

First, protection may or may not be superior to free trade
with factor price differentials. This traditional second-best argument has been made by a number of authors [24, 73, and 104,
inter alia].

Second, from a welfare viewpoint, protectionism is not the
optimal policy response to differentials. This proposition has had
an interesting history of independent rediscovery over a thirty-
year period. The proposition was made by Ohlin [175] in 1931,
restated by Meade [154] and Hagen [75] in the 1950s, and re-
discovered by Bhagwati and Ramaswami [24] in 1963. The
optimal policy is factor taxation or subsidy. To quote Ohlin: "A
cash bonus corresponding to the extra labour costs would bring
the situation closer to a more normal one, than a system of duties
can do" [175, p. 44]. Further, Ohlin noted that if the differential
is caused by factor immobility, then duties will simply increase
the differential, whereas the rational policy is "to increase the
labour mobility and do away with the watertight labour compart-
ment" [175, p. 44].

Third, policies can be ranked in terms of their efficacy in off-
setting factor price differentials. Bhagwati [23] ranks these policies
as follows:

1. First-best:   factor tax-cum-subsidy.
2. Second-best:   production tax-cum-subsidy.
3. Third-best:   tariff (trade subsidy).
4. Consumption tax-cum-subsidy will not help.

Another paper dealing with second-best-policy intervention involv-
ing distortions in the absence of international trade has been written
by Fishlow and David [60].

In response to a paper by Kemp and Negishi [119], Bhagwati
et al. [25] have written an interesting paper (a predecessor of the
paper just cited [23]). They consider the equality of the domestic
rate of transformation (DRT), the domestic rate of substitution (DRS), and the foreign rate of transformation (FRT).
They find that, if only two out of three of these are equal

under laissez faire, then there is some policy which will raise welfare, even though the equality of the first two variables is broken as a result of the policy. If all three of these variables are unequal, there is no feasible policy which will raise welfare.

Bhagwati [23], following the theory of the second-best, states that (a) reduction of a differential with other distortions in the system may not increase welfare, while (b) reduction of a differential with no other distortion in the system necessarily increases welfare. Batra and Pattanaik [14] and Foster and Sonnenschein [64] show that the second proposition is false. Batra and Pattanaik note that an increased differential with product prices fixed lowers real income, and hence welfare, when output responses are normal and increases income and welfare when output responses are perverse. This is important in that a decrease in one distortion, even with no other distortions present, does not necessarily mean an improvement in welfare. It is another consequence of multiple equilibria made possible by distortion-induced reversals of factor intensities.

In another paper, Batra and Pattanaik [12] find that a *decrease* in a country's terms of trade may lead to an *increase* in welfare if factor markets are distorted. This may have some bearing on the debate over the postwar deterioration of the terms of trade of the less developed countries since their factor markets are notoriously imperfect.

# Factor Price Rigidity and
# Factor Immobility

## 5.1  Factor Price Rigidity

Haberler [73] and Johnson [104] have discussed the introduction
of trade in an autarkic economy which is initially Pareto optimal.
In addition to trade, they added the condition that factor prices
must remain rigid at their original level. This rigidity may be caused
by a combination of institutional forces such as minimum-wage
legislation, long-term contracts, governmental regulation or control,
labor unions, or other forces. In the new equilibrium, production
of the import-competing good must cease, given the assumption
of constant returns to scale. Since all of the intensive factor in the
import-competing sector cannot be absorbed by the expansion of
the export industry, some of it will be unemployed in the new
equilibrium. The Stolper-Samuelson [217] analog is that trade
expansion has hurt a portion of the import-competing industry's
intensive factor via unemployment rather than through adverse
price changes.

The output effects can be illustrated geometrically in Fig. 5.1.
Line $L_0$ (whose slope equals $P_x/P_y$, except for sign) represents relative product prices in autarky: production and consumption occur
at $P_0$. The introduction of trade increases $P_x/P_y$ to $L_2$, moving
production to $P_2$ and consumption to $C_2$ when no distortions are
present. However, with factor price rigidity, the new production

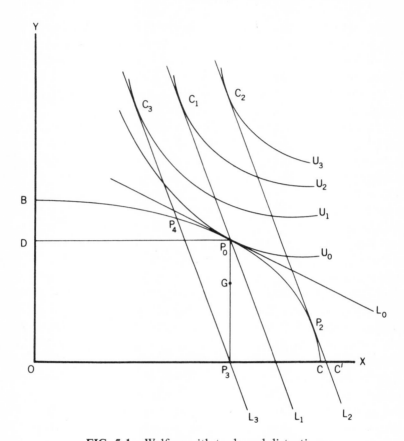

**FIG. 5.1.** Welfare with trade and distortions.

point cannot be at $P_2$ but must occur between $P_3$ and C. The
precise point may depend on which good is the numeraire because of
the index number problem. Haberler [73] and Johnson [104] conclude that free trade may actually reduce welfare in this situation.

Bardhan [10], Batra and Pattanaik [13], and Kemp [116]
have questioned these studies in their allocation of the net welfare
effects of two exogenous changes (the introduction of trade *and*
the introduction of the distortion via rigid prices) to one of the
changes alone, i.e., trade. We know that the introduction of trade

alone cannot decrease welfare, while the introduction of a distortion alone may reduce it. The effects of these two actions should be separated. Of course, no distortion is implied if factor prices are rigid because the supply of a factor is perfectly elastic at a given price (for the economy as a whole, this is precluded by our assumption of a fixed total supply of each factor).

Eckaus [53] and others have discussed the case in which fixed coefficients in the production of both goods, coupled with certain product price ratios, imply a zero price for one of the factors of production, such as labor. Societal constraints which require a nonzero wage impose a differential between the actual wage (which may be the same in all industries) and the shadow wage (which equals zero for the economy as a whole). Bhagwati [21] has used the Samuelson factor price equalization diagram to illustrate the unemployment effects of such a divergence between the actual and shadow wage in the case of a labor surplus economy in which the production functions permit smooth substitutibility. To remedy this distortion, he recommends a tax-cum-subsidy on factor use in all sectors as the first-best policy; next in order of preference would be a tax-cum-subsidy policy on the domestic production of importables or a tariff on imports.

Policy remedies aimed at factor use are also first-best in Lewis's case [135] in which wages are identical in all industries but are above the marginal product of labor in one sector—agriculture. Both shrinkage and nontangency along the transformation curve contribute to the decline in welfare which accompanies this case.

Harris and Todaro [84] have considered theoretically a more recent problem plaguing less developed countries, i.e., continued rural to urban migration in spite of positive marginal products in agriculture and substantial urban unemployment. They find that such behavior is rational, given urban minimum-wage levels above agricultural earnings, government hiring, and wage subsidies and given that migration responds to urban-rural differences in *expected* earnings. Empirically, the correlation between regions of high unemployment and high wages has been observed by Hall [78] in the United States and Bryce [37] in Panama.

## 5.2 Factor Immobility

We consider next the case in which factor prices are flexible but
the factors are immobile between industries. Cairnes [41] explored
this possibility in a one-factor model with his famous theory of
"noncompeting groups" of labor. He felt that all workers could be
classified into four skill categories [41, pp. 72-73] within which
there was perfect substitutibility but between which there was
none. An analytical solution to this problem is to divide labor into
four new factors and redefine the production functions [43, 60,
175]. Ohlin [176], however, felt that in the long run the different
qualities of labor are not necessarily separable since high wages in
skilled groups induce entry from lower-skilled categories.

On the other hand, we can also assume that there are inter-
industry barriers to labor mobility even though labor is of identical
quality in both industries in a one-factor, two-good model. By
assuming that the economy is Pareto optimal in autarky and that
factors will not move out of their autarky positions when trade is
introduced, then with trade we observe perfect factor immobility
and no change in the production of either good. Furthermore, the
Ricardian pattern of trade follows: The country exports the good
whose autarky price is less than the world price. Welfare improves
with trade in spite of the immobility. However, it would improve
still further if labor became mobile and the system were permitted
to specialize in the export product. Viner [235, p. 124] gave an
intuitive argument for the price and wage effects of trade in 1932:
"[In this case], trade between the two countries will result only in
changes in the relative prices of the two commodities, [and] in
relative wages in the two occupations. . . ."

The problem of factor immobility in two-factor models with
international trade has been investigated by Haberler [73] and
Johnson [104]. For simplicity, both assume that the country faces
a given terms of trade in world markets. They then compare a
country before and after trade to determine whether it is possible
for the country to gain from trade when its domestic factors are
completely immobile between industries. In Fig. 5.1, the country
produces and consumes at the Pareto optimal point $P_0$ in autarky.

If domestic factors are perfectly mobile, we find as before that the introduction of trade increases the price ratio $P_x/P_y$ from $L_0$ to the international terms of trade denoted by line $L_2$, production moves to $P_2$, and consumption moves to $C_2$ in the Pareto optimal equilibrium. The gain from trade is illustrated by movement from community indifference curve $U_0$ to $U_3$.

However, if factors are completely immobile, it is still possible to gain from trade. If the increase in $P_x/P_y$ from $L_0$ to $L_1$ is accompanied by flexible factor prices, then the production point remains at point $P_0$ in Fig. 5.1 and the gain from trade is from $U_0$ and $U_2$. Johnson [104, pp. 13-14] notes that the total gain from trade ($U_0$ to $U_3$) can be broken into two parts: the "consumption or exchange" gain ($U_0$ to $U_2$) and the "production or specialization" gain ($U_2$ to $U_3$). Thus, Haberler and Johnson showed, in effect, that the distortion introduced via factor immobility merely eliminates the production gain; the consumption gain remains when factor prices are flexible. The gain from trade is actually from $U_0$ to $U_3$; however, the introduction of the distortion via immobility results in a loss from $U_3$ back to $U_2$. The net effect of both the exogenous changes is the movement from $U_0$ to $U_2$.

We note the following structural effects in this case. First, both Haberler and Johnson showed that the transformation curve in Fig. 5.1 shrinks to $DP_0P_3$, so that shrinkage affects all points on the transformation curve except point $P_0$.

Second, we know that the prices of both factors in the export industry (X) increase in proportion to the change in relative commodity prices when trade is introduced. This can be shown by letting $P_x$, $P_y$ and $w_x$, $w_y$, $r_x$, $r_y$ denote commodity and factor prices in X and Y and $K_x$, $K_y$, $L_x$, $L_y$ denote the factors employed in X and Y. From the zero profit condition, it must be true that, in the long run,

$$P_x X - w_x L_x - r_x K_x = 0 \tag{5.1}$$

$$P_y Y - w_y L_y - r_y K_y = 0 \tag{5.2}$$

regardless of the mobility or immobility of the factors of

production. By assumption, $dL_x = dK_x = dL_y = dK_y = 0$, so that $L_x$, $K_x$, $L_y$, and $K_y$ are fixed. From the production functions, it must also be true that X and Y are fixed. We can then write

$$\frac{P_x}{P_y} = \frac{Y}{X} \left[ \frac{w_x L_x + r_x L_x}{w_y L_y + r_y L_y} \right] \tag{5.3}$$

Thus, if $P_x/P_y$ increases 20% when trade is introduced, the ratio of factor rewards in X relative to Y must increase by 20% [the bracketed term on the right-hand side of Eq. (5.3)]. We get the Cairnesian result that the return to these industry-specific factors are determined exclusively by changes in demand (the supply of the factors is perfectly "inelastic"). The Stolper-Samuelson [217] analog would be something like this: increased relative export prices with immobile factors benefit all factors in the export industry, instead of just the intensive factor; as a result, a constant multiplicative differential is introduced in the ratio of X's factor costs to the price of identical factor services in Y.

Thus, the structural effects are formally similar to those in the one-factor case: An identical differential is paid for the factors in the export industry; the factor market equilibrium point, by definition, remains constant; there is no shrinkage of the transformation curve at the new equilibrium point; the pattern of trade corresponds to the Heckscher-Ohlin theorem (if it would have without immobility); and the nontangency issue is irrelevant since the marginal rate of transformation is indeterminate at the corner of the transformation curve $DP_0 P_3$ at $P_0$. The case of factor immobility is important empirically; it is relevant, for example, to the problem of the "dual economy" discussed in much of the economic development literature.

## 5.3  Rigidity and Immobility

Following Johnson [104], we can combine factor *immobility* and price *rigidity* in four ways to yield the following results when trade is introduced (all are illustrated in Fig. 5.1). We assume that trade causes $P_x/P_y$ to increase from the level represented by $L_0$.

1.  If both factors are immobile and both factor prices are rigid, production of Y ceases and both of its factors are completely unemployed while production of X remains constant at point $P_3$.

2.  If both factors are immobile and the price of only one of them is rigid, then production of Y will not cease completely so that production will occur at some point such as G along the line $P_0 P_3$.

3.  If one factor is mobile with a rigid price and the other is immobile but with a flexible price, the system will arrive at a point to the right of $P_0 P_3$ and not above point G.

4.  If one factor is mobile with a flexible price and the other is immobile with a rigid price, the system will arrive at a point somewhere to the right of the line $P_0 P_3$.

These cases are also considered at some length in Batra and Pattanaik [13]. In all of the cases in which factor prices are rigid, the results depend on whether the rigid factor price is measured in terms of X, Y, or some constant utility combination of the two.

Hemming and Corden [87] have examined optimal policy alternatives in cases where output changes result in unemployment, the latter being necessary for labor movement. This work has been extended by Ramaswami [186] and Corden [48]. In another context, Ramaswami [185] examines policy-induced international factor immobility. In considering optimal restrictions on factor movements, he finds that optimal taxation of the immigration of the scarce factor is superior to optimal restriction of the emigration of the abundant factor. This was extended by Webb [239] to the case in which two governments negotiate such taxation in a bilateral monopoly situation.

## 5.4   Immobility and the Adjustment Process

Finally, Marquez-Ruarte [148], in an interesting unpublished paper, and Mayer [150] have considered the case of one mobile and one immobile factor with perfect flexibility of factor prices. They are concerned with the behavior of product markets in the "inter-run" period between the time of imposition of a tariff and the arrival of the economy at the new long-run equilibrium. If labor is perfectly mobile both in the short run and in the long run and capital is immobile in the short run but mobile in the long run, then a tariff or any price change introduces a capital differential in the import-competing industry in the short run. In the absence of reversals, the differential is eliminated as capital adjusts toward a new long-run equilibrium. The adjustment to this point occurs along what Marquez-Ruate calls an iso-price locus, corresponding to the new price. Along any short-run transformation curve (defined by a fixed capital stock and a fixed allocation of it between industries), relative product prices equal the marginal rate of transformation (so that relative price lines are *tangent* to the short-run transformation curves) since (a) the slope of the latter is determined only by marginal labor productivities, which (b) equal real wage rates, which are (c) equalized by the assumption of short-run labor mobility. This can be shown mathematically in Eq. (3.8) on p. 52. There, the term $dK_x = 0$ and wages in X and Y are identical so that $-(dY/dX) = P_x/P_y$.

The work of these two authors provides a direct application of the factor price differential model developed in Chaps. 2 and 3 to the adjustment process. Consider Fig. 2.7 on p. 31. Assume that the economy is small and increases a tariff on good Y, the importable. Capital is completely immobile in the short run, but labor is not, so that the economy moves from point S to a point directly above on the iso-price locus $X_0 HGY_0$, point Q. We assume that this iso-price locus corresponds to the new (lower) fixed price of X relative to Y. Capital moves out of X and into Y through time. As Marquez-Ruarte showed [148], the adjustment path to the new long-run equilibrium point H must be down the iso-price line QAGH. Mayer [150] noted that both capital and labor in the expanding industry might gain in the short run using this model, given certain assumptions. This result contrasts with the long-run Stolper-Samuelson result that one factor will gain and the other will lose. If only the short-run effects are considered, or if they dominate present value calculations of factor returns, then we have an explanation of labor and capital from an industry cooperating in pressing politicians for tariffs (or other measures which raise the price of the industry's output). The Stolper-Samuelson theorem is incapable of explaining such behavior.

# 6

## Empirical Studies of Distortions
## in Factor Markets

This chapter reviews briefly some empirical work on factor price differentials. This discussion is included as a supplement to the theoretical chapters and for that reason is not an exhaustive treatment. In Chap. 1 we reviewed several causes for both distortionary and nondistortionary differentials. Excellent examples of the latter are given in Mincer's survey [164]. The econometric, methodological, and measurement problems associated with measuring differentials have been investigated by Bahral [7], Hall [78], Hanna and Denison [80], Hart [85], Johansen [102], and Perlman [183]. A paper with good coverage of the pre-1962 literature has been written by Reder [190]. The studies by Clark [45, Chap. 10] and Bellerby [18] are examples of some of the applied work in the area. In this chapter we shall emphasize four topics: immobility, union power, the corporate income tax, and factor distortions with trade.

The reluctance of factors to move in response to higher real incomes may involve a quantum effect: they will not move to the higher income area or industry until the differential passes a certain threshold [176]. This inertia was demonstrated by Lester [133], who found in his survey of 48 labor market areas that the high wage to low wage ratio for identical jobs in the same community sometimes averaged 1.5. Meyers [159, p. 94] noted that "there is a good bit of evidence to show that differences between a job and no job are more effective in inducing movement of labor than differences in wages." Stafford [213] observed that unionization probably reduces geographical mobility (although Parker and Burton [181] were not able to attribute a prewar to postwar decline in U.S. mobility to unionization). Two interesting studies on migration have attempted to calculate the wage differential required to induce migration [212, 231]. Sjaastad [212] finds that in the United States "the typical migrant would be indifferent between two destinations, one of which was 146 miles more distant than the other, if the average annual labor earning were $106 higher (1947-49 dollars) in the more distant one." Vanderkamp [231] makes similar calculations for Canada, finding somewhat smaller income-distance tradeoffs. Benham et al. [19], in a study of the mobility of physicians and dentists in the United States, found that the latter are much more impeded geographically than the former because of state licensing requirements.

Marshall's work on the determinants of union power has been reviewed by Allen [2]. These determinants include an inelastic demand for the product's output, technological necessity, a low proportion of total costs attributable to labor (i.e., a capital-intensive unionized sector), and inelastic supplies of the co-operating factors. A large body of empirical work has been done on union/nonunion wage differentials in the United States, where roughly a fourth of the labor force is unionized [134, p. 5]. Many of the earlier studies on unionization are discussed in Lewis [134], which is the standard reference through 1963. Several of these studies are summarized chronologically in Table 6.1. Roughly nine estimated that unions raise union over nonunion wages, three concurred but with qualifications depending on the phase of the business cycle, five felt unions had little or no effect, and Douglas [51] found that the union-nonunion wage ratio was less than 1 and declining in the early twentieth century.

One of the most interesting results is that unions improve their position vis-a-vis nonunion labor in troughs but are hurt at peaks of the business cycle [134, 184, 218]). Thus, in addition to utilizing idle resources, high levels of employment also work to reduce distortions in labor pricing caused by contractual rigidity in

**TABLE 6.1**

**A Survey of the Effects of Unionism on Wages**

| Author | Date of study | Scope of study | Conclusions |
|---|---|---|---|
| Douglas [51] | 1930 | Real wages in U.S., 1890-1926 | In 1920, the ratio of union-non-union wages was far below the level in 1890-1899; ratio began to rise in early 1920s |
| Friedman [65] | 1951 | Comment on postwar inflation | The effect of unions on wages exaggerated; not over 10-20% of labor force affected by unions |
| Sultan [218] | 1954 | Measured ratio of share of union-nonunion (1929 = 100) between 1929 and 1951 | Unions showed relative improvement in 1931-1934, 1934-1938, 1941-1949 and declined in 1929-1931, 1939-1940, 1949-1951 |
| Locks [138] | 1955 | Investigated Cleveland, Ohio, labor market, 1945-1950 | Found greater tendency for pattern bargaining among union than non-unionized plants |
| Ulman [226] | 1955 | Comment on Friedman [65] | Unions may be able to affect the structure of wages without affecting the level of wages |
| Eisemann [54] | 1956 | Interindustry wage changes, 1939-1947 | Does not find that unions affected wage increases significantly over this period |

continued

**TABLE 6.1 (continued)**

| Author | Date of study | Scope of study | Conclusions |
|---|---|---|---|
| Maher [145] | 1956 | Used BLS data for seven industries in 1950 cross-section study | Found no significant differences in union and nonunion wages |
| Simler [211] | 1961 | Data: 1899-1954 | Found little relationship between labor's share in manufacturing industries and unionism |
| Lurie [139] | 1961 | Data for transit industry for selected years, 1920-1948 | Union over nonunion returns: 1920s 15 to 20%, early 1930s 20 to 25%, late 1930s 5 to 10%, 1940s below 18% |
| Ozanne [179] | 1962 | Occupational differentials for McCormick Works, 1858-1959 | Prosperity widens and depression narrows occupational differentials |
| Lewis [134] | 1963 | Unionism since the 1920s in the U.S. | Union-nonunion differentials highest in depressions and lowest at peaks of economic activity; union over nonunion returns: 1932 to 1933 over 25%, 1947 to 1948 less than 5% |
| Segal [209] | 1964 | Case studies | Unions are more successful with industries servicing local markets than those in national markets and with concentrated rather than competitive industries |

| | | | |
|---|---|---|---|
| Weiss [242] | 1966 | Compared union and nonunion private wage and salary income for 1959 reported in the 1/1000 sample of the 1960 census | The union-nonunion differential largely evaporates after personal characteristics of the labor force are considered |
| Stafford [213] | 1968 | Used portions of 1966 Survey of Consumer Finances gathered by the Survey Research Center, University of Michigan, to modify Weiss [142] | The union-nonunion differential is 26% for operatives, 18% for clerical and sales workers, and 0% (not statistically significant) for skilled labor (professionals, non-self-employed managers, etc.), even after personal characteristics of the labor force are considered |
| Clover [46] | 1968 | Used BLS data of 31 surveys of earnings in 23 manufacturing industries, 1960-1965 | Union wages exceeded nonunion wages by 18% although the differential narrowed somewhat over the period |
| Pierson [184] | 1968 | Combines quarterly data for U.S. manufacturing (1953-1966) into two groups: union and non-union | Average annual wage changes: union 3.62%, nonunion 2.97%, with higher profit rates in union strength closely tied to adaptability to cost of living changes; union strength has less impact in periods of low unemployment |

continued

**TABLE 6.1 (continued)**

| Author | Date of study | Scope of study | Conclusions |
|---|---|---|---|
| Throop [224] | 1968 | Cross-section data for 1950 and 1960 for two-digit manufacturing and seven other industries | Estimates that the union-nonunion wage differential increased 12.7% points 1950-1960, after allowing for skill level changes, city size, and labor supply |
| Ashenfelter [5] | 1971 | Used 1967 Survey of Economic Opportunity data for U.S. urban males (8,123 white and 3,897 black) to investigate union effects on wage discrimination | The union-nonunion wage differential is 9.7% for white males and 20.5% for black males, craft unions are more discriminatory than industrial unions, black/white male wages were 3.4% higher in 1967 than they would have been in the absence of unionism |

union wages. Fishlow and David [60, p. 534] argued, following Hagen [75], that the microeconomic "direction of [a] differential will, in general, be determined by demand conditions." To this sectoral effect we can add that they are also affected by changes in *aggregate* demand.

At this point, it is of some interest to compare the proportions of workers which are unionized by country. Table 6.2 is reproduced from Utsumi [227] and shows that the lowest percentage of the group is in the United States while the highest is in the United Kingdom and West Germany.

This chapter does not review systematically studies dealing with differentials in the returns to capital. Risk aversion is a frequently mentioned cause of such differentials. While it is not considered a welfare distortion (see, for example, Fisher's paper [59]), it has the same structural effects. In an early study, Bain [8] found that average post-tax profit rates were 12.1% in concentrated industries and 6.9% in all other industries. It is not clear what portion of these monopoly-oligopoly profits reflects differential returns to capital. Segal [209] and others have tried to establish a relationship between factor price differentials and industries which have product market power. Schwartzman [207] was unable to establish a relationship between monopoly and either high or low wages. On the other hand, Weiss [242] found relatively higher wages in concentrated industries but noted that

TABLE 6.2[a]

Percentage of Workers Unionized in Various Countries

| Country | Degree of unionization (%) | Year of measurement |
|---------|---------------------------|---------------------|
| United States | 27 to 31% | 1953 |
| Japan | 38.9% | 1955 |
| France | 40.0% | 1950 |
| West Germany | 44.2% | 1953 |
| United Kingdom | 44.6% | 1953 |

[a]Source: Utsumi [227].

this was due to the economic superiority of labor in these industries (higher productivity, embodied human capital, etc.), so that no distortion may have existed.

There is a body of rather controversial literature dealing with the incidence of the U.S. corporate income tax. If it were a tax on pure profits, there should be no attempted shifting through price, output, or factor market effects. At two extremes, Hall [77] was unable to find evidence of shifting in either the product or factor markets, while Harberger [82] found that capital bears between 112 and 120% of the tax burden, so that it distorts the factor market for capital between the corporate and noncorporate sectors. The question is complicated, however, and the variance in the two results just cited and in later studies is symptomatic of the lack of consensus in this area.

Finally, a number of studies have related differentials to international trade. A good general discussion of labor and trade is provided by Mitchell [167]. Kravis [126] found that U.S. wages in 1947 in the leading export industries were $1.46 while they were only $1.23 in import-competing industries. Keesing [115] and others have found that U.S. exports are skilled labor intensive while import-competing products use relatively large amounts of unskilled labor in their production, which helps explain Kravis' result (see also Mitchell [168]). Bourque [32] shows that import-competing industries locate primarily in the South, where skill levels are lower than the national average. Salant [197] has discussed trade and the corporate income tax, while Marx [149] argued that differentials penalize U.S. exporters relative to importers in the purchase of nonprimary inputs such as ocean freight in periods of U.S. trade balance surpluses. Several studies have examined intercountry wage differences, those of Mitchell [168] and Papola and Bharadwaj [180], to name two.

To date, I know of no empirical work which explores the theoretical question of physical and value factor intensity reversals discussed in the previous chapters. This is an important area which should be developed more fully.

# Factor Taxes, Commodity Taxes, and Welfare: A Numerical Example

## 7.1 The Model

Consider the case of a *closed* economy in which all consumers have identical and homothetic preferences and a constant marginal utility of income. The latter is an objectionable assumption on the ground that the marginal utility of income is not observable. However, the assumption of cardinal utility has been used with some success in Friedman and Savage's explanation of choice under uncertainty. It is used here for illustrative convenience. We restrict the analysis further by assuming the equality of the marginal utility of income across individuals, so that we can write a single aggregate utility function (in Cobb-Douglas form):

$$U = X^a Y^{1-a} \tag{7.1}$$

(See Johnson [109], who used this model to illustrate the welfare effects of a factor and a commodity tax on the Chicago Qualifying Examinations.) The production functions are also Cobb-Douglas:

$$X = L_x^b K_x^{1-b} \tag{7.2}$$

$$Y = L_y^c K_y^{1-c} \tag{7.3}$$

The endowment constraints are

$$L = L_x + L_y \tag{7.4}$$

$$K = K_x + K_y \tag{7.5}$$

The utility function U can be written in terms of the inputs as

$$U = L_x^{ab} K_x^{a(1-b)} L_y^{(1-a)c} K_y^{(1-a)(1-c)} \tag{7.6}$$

and the marginal utilities can be written

$$\frac{\partial U}{\partial X} = \frac{aU}{X} \qquad\qquad \frac{\partial U}{\partial Y} = \frac{(1-a)U}{Y} \tag{7.7}$$

In consumer equilibrium, there will be tangency between a utility isoquant and the economywide budget constraint, whose slope equals the ratio of product prices,

$$
\begin{aligned}
-\left(\frac{dY}{dX}\right)_{\bar{U}} &= \frac{\partial U/\partial X}{\partial U/\partial Y} \\[2mm]
&= \frac{a}{1-a}\frac{Y}{X} \\[2mm]
&= \frac{P_x}{P_y} \\[2mm]
&= (1 + t_c)\frac{dY}{dX} \\[2mm]
&= T\frac{dY}{dX}
\end{aligned}
\tag{7.8}
$$

in the case of a proportional commodity tax on good X equal to $t_c$. In the last term, $dY/dX$ is the marginal rate of transformation and reflects society's physical conversion rate of X into Y.

If there is a factor market distortion created through a factor tax on labor or a labor union in industry X, the wage in X will exceed that in Y:

$$w_x = (1 + t_f)w_y$$

$$= tw_y \tag{7.9}$$

When the marginal conditions are satisfied for factor market equilibrium, Johnson [109, p. 271] solves for national welfare levels or utility with the sales tax alone, U(T), and utility with the factor tax alone, U(t). When the ratio of these two utilities is taken, the country's endowment constraints drop out, since they are common to both cases, so that the utility ratios can be written

$$\frac{U(T)}{U(t)} = \frac{T^{1-a}}{t^{(1-a)c}} \frac{[ab + (1-a)ct]^A [a(1-b) + (1-a)(1-c)]^{1-A}}{[ab + (1-a)cT]^A [a(1-b) + (1-a)(1-c)T]^{1-A}} \tag{7.10}$$

where $A = c + a(b - c)$. In the case of no commodity tax, $T = 1$ and, with no factor tax, $t = 1$; with neither, $U(T)/U(t) = 1$.

At this point we shall depart from Johnson's question. We shall assume some values for the economic parameters and solve for utility levels under alternative tax regimes or alternative economic distortions. To make the example interesting, let X be the corporate sector in the U.S. economy and let Y be the noncorporate sector. Data for 1971 have been taken from the *Statistical Abstract* [214] to approximate the values of a, b, and c. The amount of national income originating in business was $694 billion [214, p. 378]. Of this, $469 billion was produced by corporations. A proxy for the share of corporate sector goods in final consumption [X's share in Eq. (7.1)] is a = 469/694, or

$$a = 0.68$$
$$1 - a = 0.32 \tag{7.11}$$

Of the $469 billion produced in corporations, $389 billion was employee compensation. Thus, the share of labor in value added in Eq. (7.2) is b = 389/469, or

$$b = 0.83 \quad \text{(corporate)}$$
$$1 - b = 0.17 \tag{7.12}$$

For the $225 billion of income in the noncorporate sector Y, there was employee compensation of $80 billion in sole proprietorships, $3 billion in other business, and $13 billion in government enterprises. Proprietor's income equaled $68 billion. I arbitrarily assign half of this as a return to labor ($34 billion). This gives the share of value added in Y accruing to labor in Eq. (7.3), c = 130/225, or

$$c = 0.58 \quad \text{(noncorporate)}$$
$$1 - c = 0.42 \tag{7.13}$$

The reader should be aware that the nonlabor shares reflect a composite of factor returns to capital, land, etc; for exposition convenience, we shall call this composite "capital." Relative to this composite, the corporate sector is labor intensive vis-à-vis the noncorporate sector.

## 7.2 The Welfare Effects

The welfare effects of either an endogenous distortion (such as a monopoly) in industry X or of a commodity tax on X can be analyzed together. The technique is to assume no imperfections in factor markets [let $t = 1 + t_f = 1$ in Eq. (7.10)] and solve for the utility level with the distortion T, U(T), relative to the level with no distortions, U(0). From Eq. 7.10, this yields

$$\frac{U(T)}{U(0)} = \frac{T^{1-a}[ab + (1-a)c]^A[a(1-b) + (1-a)(1-c)]^{1-A}}{[ab + (1-a)cT]^A[a(1-b) + (1-a)(1-c)T]^{1-A}} \tag{7.14}$$

[See Eq. (7.10) for a definition of A.] This formulation permits us to consider both taxes and subsidies on industry X. Since $T = 1 + t_c$, we can have T greater than, equal to, or less than 1 since $t_c$ can be greater than, equal to, or less than 0, depending on whether a tax or subsidy is indicated. In the case of monopoly market power, we are concerned only with cases in which $t_c > 0$.

Consider now a distortion in the factor market alone. A factor tax on labor in industry X or a labor union in X could be the cause of the differential. Let T = 1 in Eq. (7.10), so that the numerator U(0) represents distortions in neither product market in Eq. (7.14):

$$\frac{U(0)}{U(t)} = \frac{[ab + (1 - a)ct]^A}{t^{(1-a)c}[ab + (1 - a)c]^A} \tag{7.15}$$

We have just discussed how to calculate the welfare effects of a commodity tax on the corporate sector or of a factor tax on labor in the corporate sector. In order to generalize the simulated results, we extend this analysis to the six possible cases: commodity taxes on either the corporate or noncorporate sector; factor taxes on either capital or labor in the corporate sector; and factor taxes on either capital or labor in the noncorporate sector.

The results of these calculations are shown in Table 7.1. The numbers in parentheses in the headings of the table reflect the importance of the sectors in the utility function and the shares of value added of capital and labor in each of the sector production functions. The numbers in the table show the reduction in welfare which accompanies a tax or subsidy equal to the amount shown in column 1 of the table. For example a 30% subsidy of corporate output (–30 in column 1) results in a 1.2% reduction in welfare in the United States. Similarly, a 40% tax on corporate output also results in a 1.2% decrease in welfare. While these numbers appear to be rather small, it should be remembered that their equivalent in billions of dollars is rather large and, since they are annual flows, the total cost at any point in time is the present discounted value of these losses for as long as the tax is maintained. Thus, the present value may be quite high. Note that a tax on output of the corporate sector leads to a slightly larger loss in welfare than an equal ad valorem tax on the noncorporate sector. For the empirically relevant ranges, the losses are remarkably close, however, for equal tax rates, despite the larger size of the corporate sector.

The table can also be used for a rough approximation of the welfare cost of the corporate income tax (to the extent that it is a true tax on nonwage income in the corporate sector). The effective

## TABLE 7.1

### Percent Reductions in Welfare (U) for Alternative Taxes and Subsidies in the United States

| Percent tax (<0, subsidy) | Corporate taxed sector (0.68) | | | Noncorporate taxed sector (0.32) | | |
|---|---|---|---|---|---|---|
| | Commodity tax | Factor tax on | | Commodity tax | Factor tax on | |
| | | Capital (0.17) | Labor (0.83) | | Capital (0.42) | Labor (0.58) |
| -90 | 31.8 | 13.4 | 21.2 | 44.2 | 12.3 | 36.3 |
| -80 | 18.9 | 7.3 | 12.5 | 25.0 | 6.8 | 19.5 |
| -70 | 11.7 | 4.3 | 7.8 | 14.8 | 4.1 | 11.2 |
| -60 | 7.3 | 2.5 | 4.8 | 8.7 | 2.4 | 6.5 |
| -50 | 4.4 | 1.5 | 2.9 | 5.0 | 1.4 | 3.7 |
| -40 | 2.4 | 0.8 | 1.6 | 2.7 | 0.8 | 2.0 |
| -30 | 1.2 | 0.4 | 0.8 | 1.3 | 0.4 | 0.9 |
| -20 | 0.5 | 0.2 | 0.3 | 0.5 | 0.2 | 0.4 |
| -10 | 0.1 | 0.0 | 0.1 | 0.1 | 0.0 | 0.1 |
| 0 | 0.0 | 0.0 | 0.0 | 0.0 | 0.0 | 0.0 |
| 10 | 0.1 | 0.0 | 0.1 | 0.1 | 0.0 | 0.1 |
| 20 | 0.3 | 0.1 | 0.2 | 0.3 | 0.1 | 0.2 |
| 30 | 0.7 | 0.2 | 0.5 | 0.7 | 0.2 | 0.5 |
| 40 | 1.2 | 0.3 | 0.8 | 1.1 | 0.4 | 0.7 |
| 50 | 1.7 | 0.5 | 1.2 | 1.6 | 0.5 | 1.1 |
| 60 | 2.3 | 0.7 | 1.6 | 2.1 | 0.7 | 1.4 |
| 70 | 2.9 | 0.9 | 2.1 | 2.6 | 0.9 | 1.8 |
| 80 | 3.6 | 1.0 | 2.6 | 3.2 | 1.1 | 2.1 |
| 90 | 4.3 | 1.2 | 3.1 | 3.8 | 1.3 | 2.5 |
| 100 | 5.0 | 1.4 | 3.7 | 4.4 | 1.5 | 2.9 |

corporate tax rate is somewhere between 30 and 40%. According to the third column in the table, this indicates a reduction of between 0.2 and 0.3% in national welfare (assuming no other distortions). In 1971, this is equivalent to a decline in national income originating in business of between $1.4 billion and $2.1 billion. Of course, the relevant consideration is the tax on capital in the corporate sector relative to the noncorporate sector. If these relative tax rates are only one-half the 30 to 40% range given earlier, then the welfare cost is only one-half the numbers just stated.

The table can also be used to analyze product market distortions. For example, if the noncorporate sector were perfectly competitive while the corporate sector were sufficiently noncompetitive so that market prices were 10% above actual resource costs, then national welfare would decline by 0.1%. In general, the table illustrates that a factor tax in either sector leads to a larger welfare decline the larger the share of that factor in value added. The same is true of commodity taxes but it not true of commodity subsidies. That is, for the case considered, equal percent subsidies in the two sectors result in a larger decline in income if the subsidy is on the small sector.

## 7.3 The Iso-Welfare "Loss" Function

Given the results of the previous two sections, it is clear that, in the case considered here, a commodity tax results in a larger welfare loss than an equivalent ad valorem tax on one of the factors. We can construct an "iso-utility loss" locus or "iso-loss function" which plots alternative levels of the two taxes which give equivalent welfare losses. For example if $t_c = 0.30$ and $t_f = 0.35$ is a point on the curve, it means that a commodity tax alone of 30% (with no other taxes present, including a factor tax) would give the same welfare loss as a 35% tax on a specified factor (again, with no other taxes present).

This locus can be derived by inserting arbitrary values of T into Eq. (7.14) and solving for the value of t in Eq. (7.15) which gives the same percentage reduction in utility. Since both taxes and subsidies give welfare losses, it is clear that

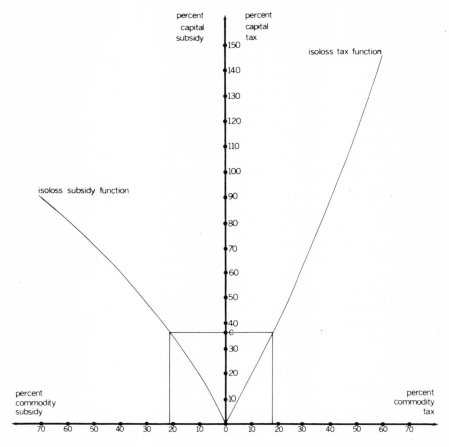

**FIG. 7.1.** Iso-loss functions for alternative commodity and capital taxes (subsidies) in the corporate sector.

there will be at least two values of T (one positive and one negative) which could be assigned to any arbitrary T.

Both iso-loss tax functions and iso-loss subsidy functions can be constructed. These are shown in Fig. 7.1 for alternative commodity and capital taxes (subsidies) in the corporate sector. Because of the small share of capital in value added, the functions rise rather steeply. At relatively low levels, the ratio of the capital to commodity tax which gives the same welfare distortion is roughly 2 to 1 (a 20% capital tax is equivalent to a 10% commodity tax) while the ratio increases at very high rates (a 140% capital tax is equivalent to a 57% commodity tax).

The iso-loss *subsidy* function exhibits nearly uniform concavity (from below). In terms of levels, an 80% capital subsidy is welfare equivalent to a 60% commodity subsidy. The lines drawn in at a capital tax-subsidy level of 35%, which was our earlier estimate of the effective rate of the corporate income tax, indicates the following. A 35% capital tax is equivalent to an 18% commodity tax and a 21% commodity subsidy on corporate output.

This chapter also illustrates the danger of using "rule-of-thumb" estimates for the welfare effects of alternative distortions in general equilibrium. For example, since the corporate sector is over twice as large as the noncorporate sector in the example considered (68 percent vs. 32 percent), there is a temptation to say that a tax on corporate output might be about twice as distortionary as an equivalent tax on noncorporate output. However, Table 7.1 shows that a 50 percent tax on the noncorporate sector yields a welfare loss of 1.6 percent while a 50 percent tax on the corporate sector yields a loss of only 1.7 percent. Thus, partial equilibrium rules of thumb do not always carry over to general equilibrium situations. They must be used with care.

# 8

## Summary

This chapter provides an overview of the results of the book. In the first chapter, we note that factor price differentials may be due to unobservable economic factors such as human capital, risk aversion, etc. A factor price differential may or may not imply that a welfare loss is involved. Differentials which arise out of short-run disequilibrium are eliminated in the long run as factor market arbitrage occurs. In cases in which welfare distortions are involved it is not necessarily true that government action should be mobilized to eliminate the differential. The question hinges on the present discounted value of eliminating the differential through government action relative to the present value of the costs of the government action.

In Sec. 2.1, we note the Hagen result that free trade may not be the optimal policy in the presence of a domestic distortion and Samuelson's extension of the two-product, one-factor model to the multiproduct case. We explore the way in which comparative advantage can be explained using the Mangoldt-Edgeworth technique with distortions present. The results show that any pattern of trade is possible, given the appropriate wage differentials on the single factor, labor.

In Sec. 2.2, we develop the two-factor, two-commodity model with a distortion in one of the factor markets. "Iso-distortion loci" and "iso-price loci" are used to analyze factor market distortions in the Edgeworth-Bowley box. The general equilibrium model constructed in Sec. 2.2 includes both the supply and the demand for goods and factors in a small country facing a fixed world terms of trade.

In Sec. 2.3, we stress the distinction between the *physical* factor intensities of products and the *value* factor intensities. The physical factor intensities are defined in terms of the capital-labor ratios, while the value factor intensities are defined in terms of the relative shares of output going to each of the two factors in the two industries. While this distinction is not important in the traditional case in which all economic activity occurs along the nondistorted efficiency locus in the Edgeworth-Bowley box, it is an important distinction when we analyze all other possible equilibrium points in the box. We note that physical factor intensities can be reversed only if an industry pays the differential for its physically intensive factor. Value factor intensities cannot reverse between the nondistorted efficiency locus and the diagonal in the Edgeworth-Bowley box. For completely general production functions, however, it may be possible that value reversals occur in all other parts of the box (i.e., on both sides of the diagonal).

In Sec. 2.4, we deal with the factor market effects of a factor price differential. The results indicate that when the physical and the value factor intensities of a product correspond (the "normal" case), if industry X must pay a higher differential for capital, then the capital-labor ratio actually *increases* both in the X industry and in the Y industry if capital is the intensive factor in X. The capital-labor ratios decrease if capital is not the intensive factor in X. Some paradoxical results are generated in this situation. If a factor in the first industry obtains market power and attempts to increase the differential which it receives in the first industry over the price it receives in the other industry, then in the new equilibrium, general equilibrium effects cause the factor to be worse off in both industries than if it had not exerted its market power. The implications are that labor unions, for example, would be better off by establishing a wage differential in the industry in which it is the nonintensive factor rather than the intensive factor of production. The numbers discussed in Chap. 7 indicate that the corporate sector in the United States is much more labor intensive than the noncorporate sector. If this is true, and if the assumptions of the model hold, then one wonders whether labor unions in the corporate sector have been a positive or negative contribution to real income of union labor.

Another important result is that, for the small country which faces a fixed world terms of trade, it is impossible for factor price differentials, no matter how large, to reverse the physical factor intensities of the products. The reason is that complete specialization is reached before reversals can occur. Another result is that the Stolper-Samuelson theorem can be generalized to hold for all interior points in the Edgeworth-Bowley box if factor intensities are stated in terms of the value rather than of the physical factor intensities of the product.

The effects of an increased factor price differential on an industry are broken into three parts in Sec. 2.4: the substitution effect, the output effect, and the price effect. If we hold output and prices constant, an increased differential which the X industry must pay for capital will result in a substitution effect away from capital. If the industry is capital intensive, permitting output to decline because of decreased profits in the X industry, it contributes, ceteris paribus, to an increase in the capital-labor ratio in the X industry if X is capital intensive (and the reverse when it is labor intensive). We show that in the normal case, when the substitution effect and the output effects work in opposite directions, the output effect will always dominate the substitution effect. This explains the paradox of an increased capital differential in the X industry resulting in an ultimate increase in the capital-labor ratio in the X industry. If we relax the assumption that the country faces a fixed international terms of trade, so that relative product prices can change as a result of the differential, then the decline in the output of the industry paying the differential will result in an increase in the relative price of its product and this change will contribute also to the change in the capital-labor ratios. In the paradoxical case just considered, the increase in the relative price of X will provide a partial or total offset to the net output effect. If demand is sufficiently inelastic, the paradox evaporates and our partial equilibrium intuition correctly predicts that an increased capital differential paid by X leads to a decrease in the capital-labor ratio in X and an increase in Y.

In Sec. 2.5, the output effects of differentials are considered. While it is ambiguous mathematically that a changed differential will cause the output of one good to increase and the other to decrease, it is not ambiguous geometrically. The mathematics show that the capital-labor ratios of the two industries will always move in the same direction in the small-country case. Geometrically, this dictates that the output effects be unambiguously positive for one good and negative for the other. This result holds for all possible points in the Edgeworth-Bowley box and all possible combinations of value and physical factor intensities.

In Sec. 2.6, we note that the Rybczynski growth results are unaffected when a factor price differential exists in factor markets. That is, an exogenous input of capital will result in no change in the equilibrium capital-labor ratios in both industries as long as there is nonspecialization in production, an increase in output of the good which is physically capital intensive and a decrease in the output of the other. The slope of the Rybczynski line is negative, as in the nondistorted case.

In Sec. 2.7, we discuss the general result that an increase in a differential or a decrease in the relative price of a product will result in a decrease in its output and "normal" supply behavior if the physical and the value factor intensities correspond while the reverse holds when they do not. Since either of the two factor intensities may reverse when compared with the nondistorted case, there are four possible cases: in two cases we get normal supply effects and in two cases we get abnormal supply effects. In the abnormal case, the supply curve of output is negatively sloped when plotted against its relative price.

Section 2.8 shows how the standard Sameulson-Johnson factor price equalization diagram can be modified to take account of factor price differentials. In Sec. 2.9, we note the likelihood of physical and value factor intensity reversals. As noted earlier, physical factor intensities can reverse only if one of the industries pays a differential for its intensive factor. In this case, the differential required for a physical reversal generally becomes smaller the higher the elasticities of factor substitution and the more similar the initial factor intensities of the products.

It is more difficult to generalize on the likelihood of value factor intensity reversals. For Cobb-Douglas production functions, value factor intensity reversals are impossible since the distributive shares in each industry are invariant to changes in either relative product prices or factor prices. In the case in which physical factor intensities have not been reversed, the value intensities can reverse only if an industry pays a differential on its nonintensive factor. Two other conditions are derived which are sufficient to determine whether value intensities will reverse. In Sec. 2.10, an endogenous differential is discussed.

Chapter 3 deals with differentials, prices, and the transformation schedule. In Sec. 3.1, a simple geometric technique is developed providing derivation of the production possibility curve, both with and without differentials. Section 3.2 deals with the shrinkage of the production possibility curve and the nonequivalence of the market prices for goods and the marginal rate at which the economy can transform one good into another (i.e., the *shrinkage* and the *nontangency* effects). The results indicate that a single differential on one factor in one of the industries yields both shrinkage and nontangency. An identical differential paid on all factors in a given industry results in no shrinkage of the transformation curve, but it does lead to nontangency between the relative market prices and the marginal rate of transformation. This would occur, for example, if both capital and labor received a 20% higher return in one industry than in another. In still another case, if one industry pays a differential for labor while the other pays a differential for capital, then the shrinkage problem is accentuated while the nontangency phenomenon is reduced (and in a very special case eliminated). The discussion of the shape of the transformation curve in Sec. 3.3 notes that differentials can cause the transformation curve to become convex from below. While we might presume that supply responses to price changes would be perverse in a convex region of the transformation curve, there is no theoretical reason why this should be the case. Normal supply response is possible along convex portions and perverse response is possible along concave portions of the transformation curve.

Section 3.4 illustrates the proposition that, in order for physical factor intensities to reverse and for the nonspecialized factor market equilibrium to move from one side of the diagonal in the Edgeworth-Bowley box to the other side, both the differential and the relative price of the industry paying the differential must increase (recall that the differential must be on its intensive factor). We also note that this result is an implication of the more general proposition that the set of all relative prices which permit non-specialized factor market equilibrium below the diagonal in the Edgeworth-Bowley box is mutually exclusive of the set of relative product prices giving equilibrium above the diagonal. In the case of linearly homogeneous production functions, there is a unique value of both the factor price differential and relative product prices at which physical factor intensities reverse. These unique values form upper bounds on the set of differentials and relative product prices in one set and a lower bound on the other set.

Chapter 4 deals with international trade, factor movements, and welfare with differentials. Section 4.1 notes that an increase in a differential paid by the import-competing industry on either factor increases both exports and imports, moving the country away from trade reversal. The pattern of trade can reverse only in the case in which the export industry pays a differential (on either factor). Thus, factor price differentials have a direct effect on the importance of trade in a national economy (i.e., the share of trade in gross national product). If the Heckscher-Ohlin theorem correctly predicts the pattern of trade before trade reversal, then it will obviously fail to explain the pattern of trade if a factor price differential has caused the trade pattern to reverse. This proposition holds regardless of whether we use the physical or the pretrade factor price ratios as definitions of relative factor abundance. An important result is that if we permit all possible cases to be considered (trade reversals, physical intensity reversals, and value intensity reversals), then the Edgeworth-Bowley box can be divided into eight possible regions. Anyone attempting to test the Heckscher-Ohlin theorem empirically would find that the theorem holds in four regions and that it does not (the Leontief-type result) in the other four regions. Furthermore, four of the eight regions (two of the Heckscher-Ohlin regions and two of the Leontief regions) switch their pattern of confirmation or nonconfirmation of the theorem if the person doing the test switches his definition of factor intensities (from physical to value or vice-versa). This results from the lack of correspondence between the physical and the value factor intensities in four of the regions.

Consider the implications of differentials for factor prices and the desire of factors to move internationally. Starting from a situation in which no reversal of any kind has occurred, if the export industry pays the differential, the price of the country's physically abundant factor in both industries will be below the price in non-distorted factor markets abroad, even with free trade in products. If the import-competing industry pays the differential, the price of the country's physically abundant factor in both industries will be above the price in nondistorted foreign markets. In the last case, we get the paradoxical result of factors wanting to move from countries where they are already scarce to countries where they are abundant. With tariffs introduced, it is possible to get international capital cross flows, i.e., domestic capital will want to emigrate from the X industry while foreign capital will want to enter the Y industry, given the distorted home factor markets.

Section 4.3 discusses trade and welfare in the presence of factor market distortions. The usual presumption is that the reduction of a factor price differential with no other distortion in the system increases welfare. However, this has been shown to be false since when output responses are perverse, an increased differential may increase income and welfare. The usual results hold in the normal case.

Chapter 5 deals with factor price rigidity and factor mobility. The analysis deals with effects of these factors on output. The immobility question is discussed in the context of both one-factor and two-factor models. In the case of immobility, the adjustment paths of factor markets to exogenous shocks are described.

Chapter 6 deals with empirical studies of distortions in factor markets. This includes reviews of studies of mobility, how union power varies over the business cycle, and the degree of unionization in the United States and a number of foreign countries.

Chapter 7 provides a numerical example of the effects of both factor taxes and commodity taxes on welfare in a closed economy. A cardinal Cobb-Douglas utility function and Cobb-Douglas production functions are used in the calculations. In order to make the example interesting and realistic, the parameters on the utility function and production functions are chosen from U.S. 1971 data. The economy is broken up into two sectors: corporate and noncorporate. The results indicate that the welfare effects of a commodity tax in the corporate sector of 20%, or a capital tax in the corporate sector of 40%, or a factor tax on labor in the corporate sector of approximately 22% would all yield welfare declines in the United States of approximately 0.3%. The final section, 7.3, develops iso-welfare loss functions which give alternative levels of commodity taxes and factor taxes which would yield equivalant welfare losses. In a comparison of the corporate income tax (assumed to fall entirely on the returns to capital) and a commodity tax on the corporate sector, the iso-loss function indicates that, for alternative levels of the corporate income tax, a commodity tax of approximately half the corporate income tax level yields equivalent welfare losses. The results also indicate that an effective corporate income tax of 35% would yield a reduction in U.S. welfare every year of 0.25%.

Chapter 7 also shows the alarming inaccuracy which is possible when partial equilibrium rules of thumb are used to estimate the general equilibrium effects of distortions on welfare.

# References

1. Adams, F. C., "The Size of Individual Incomes: Socioeconomic Variables and Chance Variation," *Review of Economics and Statistics, 40* (November 1958), pp. 390-398.
2. Allen, Bruce T., "Market Concentration and Wage Increases, 1947-1964," *Industrial and Labor Relations Review, 21* (April 1968), pp. 353-366.
3. Altman, Stuart H., and Fisher, Anthony C., "Marginal Product of Labor, Wages and Disequilibrium: Comment," *Review of Economics and Statistics, 51* (November 1969), pp. 485-486.
4. Arrow, K. J., Chenery, H. B., Minhas, B. S., and Solow, R. M., "Capital-Labor Substitution and Economic Efficiency," *Review of Economics and Statistics, 43* (August 1961), pp. 225-250.
5. Ashenfelter, Orley, "Racial Discrimination and Trade Unionism," Working Paper No. 17 revised, Princeton, N. J.: Industrial Relations Section, Princeton University, 1971.
6. Auerbach, Robert, "The Effects of Price Supports on Output and Factor Prices in Agriculture," *Journal of Political Economy, 78* (November/December 1970), pp. 1355-1361.
7. Bahral, Uri, "Wage Differentials and Specification Bias in Estimates of Relative Labor Prices," *Review of Economics and Statistics, 44* (November 1962), pp. 473-481.
8. Bain, J. S., "Relation of Profit Rate to Industry Concentration: American Manufacturing, 1936-1940," *Quarterly Journal of Economics, 65* (August 1951), pp. 293-324.

113

9. Balassa, Bela, "Trade Liberalization and 'Revealed' Comparative Advantage," *Manchester School of Economic and Social Studies, 33* (May 1965), pp. 99-123.

10. Bardhan, P. K., "Factor Market Disequilibrium and the Theory of Protection," *Oxford Economic Papers, 16* (November 1964), pp. 375-388.

11. Batra, R., "Factor Accumulation and the Terms of Trade: A Three-Country, Three-Commodity, Three-Factor Analysis," *Econometrica, 38* (May 1970), pp. 449-452.

12. Batra, R., and Pattanaik, P. K., "Domestic Distortions and the Gains from Trade," *Economic Journal, 80* (September 1970), pp. 638-649.

13. Batra, R., and Pattanaik, P. K., "Factor Market Imperfections and Gains from Trade," *Oxford Economic Papers, 23* (July 1971), pp. 182-188.

14. Batra, R., and Pattanaik, P. K., "Factor Market Imperfections, the Terms of Trade and Welfare," *American Economic Review, 61* (December 1971), pp. 946-955.

15. Behman, Sara, "Wage Changes, Institutions and Relative Factor Prices in Manufacturing," *Review of Economics and Statistics, 51* (August 1969), pp. 227-238.

16. Bell, Duran, "Occupational Discrimination as a Source of Income Differences: Lessons of the 1960's," *American Economic Review, 62* (May 1972), pp. 363-372.

17. Bell, Frederick W., "The Effect of Monopoly Profits and Wages on Prices and Consumers' Surplus in U. S. Manufacturing," *Western Economic Journal, 6* (June 1968), pp. 233-241.

18. Bellerby, J. R., ed., *Agriculture and Industry Relative Income.* London: Macmillan, 1956.

19. Benham, Lee, Maurizi, Alex, and Reder, Melvin W., "Migration, Location and Remuneration of Medical Personnel: Physicians and Dentists," *Review of Economics and Statistics, 50* (August 1968), pp. 332-347. Reprinted in John F. Burton, Jr., Lee K. Benham, William M. Vaugh III, and Robert J. Flanagan, *Readings in Labor Market Analysis.* New York: Holt, Rinehart and Winston, 1971.

20. Bhagwati, Jagdish, "The Pure Theory of International Trade: A Survey," *Economic Journal, 74* (March 1964), pp. 1-84. An addendum to the survey has been publsihed in J. Bhagwati, *Trade, Tariffs and Growth.* Cambridge, Mass.: MIT Press, 1969, pp. 99-109.

21. Bhagwati, Jagdish, *The Theory and Practice of Commercial Policy,* Frank Graham Memorial Lecture (1967), Special Papers in International Economics No. 8. Princeton, N. J.: Princeton University, 1968.

22. Bhagwati, Jagdish, "Distortions and Immiserizing Growth: A General-ization," *Review of Economic Studies, 35* (November 1968), pp. 481-485.
23. Bhagwati, Jagdish, "The Generalized Theory of Distortions and Welfare," in *Trade, Balance of Payments and Growth* (J. Bhagwati *et al.*, eds.), Papers in International Economics in Honor of Charles P. Kindleberger. Amsterdam: North Holland, 1971, pp. 69-90.
24. Bhagwati, J., and Ramaswami, V. K., "Domestic Distortions, Tariffs and the Theory of Optimum Subsidy," *Journal of Political Economy, 71* (February 1963), pp. 44-50.
25. Bhagwati, J., Ramaswami, V. K., and Srinivasan, T. N., "Domestic Distortions, Tariffs and the Theory of Optimum Subsidy: Some Further Results," *Journal of Political Economy, 77* (September 1969), pp. 1005-1010.
26. Bhagwati, J., and Srinivasan, T. N., "Optimal Policy Intervention to Achieve Noneconomic Objectives," *Review of Economic Studies, 36* (January 1969), pp. 27-38.
27. Bhagwati, J., and Srinivasan, T. N., "The Theory of Wage Differentials: Production Response and Factor Price Equalization," *Journal of International Economics, 1* (February 1971), pp. 19-35.
28. Bharadwaj, R., "Factor Proportions and the Structure of Indo-U.S. Trade," *Indian Economic Journal, 10* (October 1962), pp. 105-116.
29. Black, J., "Foreign Trade and Real Wages," *Economic Journal, 79* (March 1969), pp. 184-185.
30. Boskin, Michael J., "Unions and Relative Real Wages," *American Economic Review, 62* (June 1972), pp. 466-472.
31. Bottomley, Anthony, and Nudds, Donald, "Factor Pricing with Unlimited Supplies of Labour," *Manchester School of Economics and Social Studies, 35* (September 1967), pp. 277-284.
32. Bourque, P. J., "Geographic Earnings Differentials and Foreign Trade," *Review of Economics and Statistics, 40* (May 1958), pp. 177-179.
33. Brecx, Paul, "Leontief's Paradox," *Review of Economics and Statistics, 49* (November 1967), pp. 603-607.
34. Bronfenbrenner, M., "Wages in Excess of Marginal Revenue Product," *Southern Economic Journal, 16* (January 1950), pp. 297-309.
35. Bronfenbrenner, M., "Potential Monopsony in Labor Markets," *Industrial and Labor Relations Review, 9* (July 1956), pp. 577-588.
36. Brozen, Yale, "Minimum Wage Rates and Household Workers,"

*Journal of Law and Economics, 5* (October 1962), pp. 103-109.

37. Bryce, Herrington, J., "Regional Labor Earnings Differentials in a Small Developing Country: The Republic of Panama," *Journal of Regional Science, 9* (December 1969), pp. 405-415.

38. Buchanon, Norman S., "Lines on the Leontief Paradox," *Economia Internazionale, 8* (November 1955), ppl 791-794.

39. Burman, George R., "The Economics of Discrimination: The Impact of Public Policy," unpublished Ph.D. dissertation. Chicago: Graduate School of Business, University of Chicago, 1973.

40. Burton, John F., Jr., Benham, Lee K., Vaughn, William M., III, and Flanagan, Robert J., eds., *Readings in Labor Market Analysis.* New York: Holt, Rinehart and Winston, 1971.

41. Cairnes, J. E., *Some Leading Principles of Political Economy.* London: Macmillan, 1874.

42. Casas, F. R., "International Trade and Economic Growth in the Presence of Factor Market Distortions," *The American Economist, 16* (Spring 1972), pp. 112-119.

43. Caves, Richard, *Trade and Economic Structure.* Cambridge, Mass.: Harvard University Press, 1960, pp. 58-68.

44. Chacholiades, Miltiades, "Increasing Returns and Comparative Advantage," *Southern Economic Journal, 37* (October 1970), pp. 157-162.

45. Clark, Colin, *The Conditions of Economic Progress.* London: Macmillan. 1957.

46. Clover, Vernon T., "Compensation in Union and Nonunion Plants, 1960-1965," *Industrial and Labor Relations Review, 21* (January 1968), pp. 226-234.

47. Corden, W. M., *Recent Developments in the Theory of International Trade.* Princeton, N. J.: International Finance Section, Department of Economics, Princeton University, 1965.

48. Corden, W. M., "Wage Rigidity and the Balance of Payments: A Third-Best Argument for Tariffs?" unpublished, Oxford University, 1971.

49. Despres, E., and Kindleberger, C. P., "The Mechanism for Adjustment in International Payments—The Lessons of Post-War Experience," *American Economic Review, 42* (May 1952), pp. 332-344.

50. Diab, Muhammed, The United States Capital Position and the Structure of Foreign Trade. Amsterdam: North Holland, 1956.

51. Douglas, P. H., *Real Wages in the United States, 1890-1926.* Boston: Houghton-Mifflin, 1930.

52. Eagley, R. V., "Market Power as an Intervening Mechanism in Phillips

Curve Analysis," *Economica, New Series, 32* (February 1965), pp. 48-64.

53. Eckaus, R. S., "The Factor Proportions Problem in Underdeveloped Areas," in *The Economics of Underdevelopment* (A. N. Agarwale and S. P. Singh, eds.). New York: Oxford University Press, 1963, pp. 348-378. Reprinted from the *American Economic Review, 45* (September 1955), pp. 539-565.

54. Eisemann, D. M., "Inter-Industry Wage Changes, 1939-1947," *Review of Economics and Statistics, 38* (November 1956), pp. 445-448.

55. Elliott, G. A., "Comment," *Review of Economics and Statistics, 60* (Supplement, February 1958), pp. 116-117.

56. Estle, Edwin F., "A More Conclusive Regional Test of the Heckscher-Ohlin Hypothesis," *Journal of Political Economy, 75* (December 1967) pp. 886-888.

57. Fellner, William, and Haley, Bernard F., *A.E.A. Readings in the Theory of Income Distribution,* Homewood, Ill.: Richard D. Irwin, 1951.

58. Findlay, Ronald, *Trade and Specialization,* London: Penguin, 1970.

59. Fisher, L., "Determinants of Risk Premiums on Corporate Bonds," *Journal of Political Economy, 67* (June 1959), pp. 217-237.

60. Fishlow, Albert, and David, Paul A., "Optimal Resource Allocation in an Imperfect Market Setting," *Journal of Political Economy, 69* (December 1961), pp. 529-546.

61. Fogel, W. A., "Job Rate Ranges: A Theoretical and Empirical Analysis," *Industrial and Labor Relations Review, 17* (July 1964), pp. 584-597.

62. Forchheimer, Karl, "The Role of Relative Wage Differences in International Trade," *Quarterly Journal of Economics, 62* (November 1947), pp. 1-30.

63. Ford, James L., "The Ohlin-Heckscher Theory of the Basis of Commodity Trade," *Economic Journal, 73* (September 1963), pp. 458-476.

64. Foster, Edward, and Sonnenschein, Hugo, "Price Distortion and Economic Welfare, *Econometrica, 38* (March 1970), pp. 281-297.

65. Friedman, Milton, "Some Comments on the Significance of Labor Unions for Economic Policy," in *The Impact of the Union* (David M. Wright, ed.). New York: Harcourt Brace, 1951, pp. 204-234.

66. Fuchs, Victor R., and Perlman, Richard, "Recent Trends in Southern Wage Differentials," *Review of Economics and Statistics, 42* (August 1960), pp. 292-300.

67. Fukuchi, Takao, and Nobukuni, Makoto, "An Econometric Analysis

of National Growth and Regional Income Equality," *International Economic Review, 11* (February 1970), pp. 84-100.

68. Gallaway, Lowell, "The North-South Wage Differential," *Review of Economic Statistics, 45* (August 1965), pp. 264-277.

69. Garbarino, Joseph, "A Theory of Interindustry Wage Structure Variation," *Quarterly Journal of Economics, 64* (May 1950), pp. 282-305.

70. Gerakis, Andreas S., "A Geometrical Note on the Bochs Diagram," *Economica, New Series, 28* (August 1961), pp. 310-313.

71. Grubel, Herbert G., "Intra-Industry Specialization and the Pattern of Trade," *Canadian Journal of Economics and Political Science, 33* (August 1967), pp. 374-388.

72. Haberler, Gottfried, *The Theory of International Trade.* New York: Macmillan, 1937.

73. Haberler, Gottfried, "Some Problems in the Pure Theory of International Trade," *Economic Journal, 60* (June, 1950), pp. 223-240. Reprinted in *A.E.A. Readings in International Economics* (R. E. Caves and H. G. Johnson, eds.). Homewood, Ill.: Richard D. Irwin, 1968, pp. 213-229.

74. Haberler, Gottfried, "Real Cost, Money Cost and Comparative Advantage," *International Social Science Bulletin, 3* (Spring 1951), pp. 54-58.

75. Hagen, Everett E., "An Economic Justification of Protectionism," *Quarterly Journal of Economics, 72* (November 1958), pp. 496-514.

76. Hagen, Everett E., "Reply," *Quarterly Journal of Economics, 75* (February 1961), pp. 145-151.

77. Hall, Challis A., "Direct Shifting of the Corporation Income Tax in Manufacturing," *American Economic Review, 54* (May 1964), pp. 258-271.

78. Hall, Robert E., "Why Is the Unemployment Rate So High at Full Employment?" *Brookings Papers on Economic Activity, 3* (1970), pp. 369-410.

79. Hamada, H., "On the Optimal Transfer and Income Distribution in a Growing Economy," *Review of Economic Studies, 34* (July 1967), pp. 295-299.

80. Hanna, Frank A. (and E. F. Denison's comment), "Analysis of Interstate Income Differentials: Theory and Practice," in Conference on Research in Income and Wealth, *Regional Income (Studies in Income and Wealth,* Vol. 21). Princeton, N. J.: Princeton University Press (for the National Bureau of Economic Research), 1957, pp. 113-179.

81. Hanoch, Giora, "An Economic Analysis of Earnings and Schooling," *Journal of Human Resources, 2* (Summer 1967), pp. 310-329.

82. Harberger, Arnold C., "The Incidence of the Corporation Tax," *Journal of Political Economy, 70* (June 1962), pp. 215-240.

83. Harcourt, G. C., "Some Cambridge Controversies in the Theory of Capital," *Journal of Economic Literature, 7* (June 1969), pp. 369-405.

84. Harris, J. R., and Todaro, M. P., "Migration, Unemployment and Development: A Two-Sector Analysis," *American Economic Review, 60* (March 1970), pp. 126-142.

85. Hart, P. E., "Statistical Measures of Concentration vs. Concentration Ratios," *Review of Economics and Statistics, 43* (February 1961), pp. 85-86.

86. Heckscher, Eli, "The Effect of Foreign Trade on the Distribution of Income," *Ekonomisk Tidskrift, 21* (1919), pp. 497-512. Reprinted in *Readings in the Theory of International Trade* (H. S. Ellis and L. A. Metzler, eds.). Homewood, Ill.: Richard D. Irwin, 1949, pp. 272-300.

87. Hemming, M. F. W., and Corden, W. M., "Import Restrictions as an Instrument of Balance of Payments Policy," *Economic Journal, 68* (September 1958), pp. 483-510.

88. Henderson, A., "The Restriction of Foreign Trade," *Manchester School of Economics and Social Studies, 17* (January 1949), pp. 12-35.

89. Henderson, John P., "An Intercity Comparison of Differentials in Earnings and the City Worker's Cost of Living," *Review of Economic Statistics, 37* (November 1955), pp. 407-411.

90. Herberg, Horst, "On a Two-Sector Model with Non-Shiftable Capital and Labour-Market Imperfections," unpublished, 1971.

91. Herberg, Horst, and Kemp, Murray C., "Factor Market Distortions, the Shape of the Locus of Competitive Outputs and the Relation Between Product Prices and Equilibrium Outputs," in *Trade, Balance of Payments and Growth* (J. Bhagwati *et al.,* eds.), Papers in International Economics in Honor of Charles P. Kindleberger. Amsterdam: North Holland, 1971, pp. 22-48.

92. Herberg, Horst, and Kemp, Murray C., "Growth and Factor Market 'Imperfection,' " *Zeitschrift Fur Die Gesamte Staatswissenschaft, 128* (November 1972), pp. 590-604.

93. Herberg, Horst, and Kemp, Murray C., "On Neoclassical Growth with Permanent Factor Market Imperfections," unpublished, 1972.

94. Herberg, Horst, Kemp, Murray C., and Magee, Stephen P., "Factor Market Distortions, the Reversal of Relative Factor Intensities, and the Relation Between Product Prices and Equilibrium Outputs," *Economic Record, 47* (December 1971), pp. 518-530.

95. Hieser, R. O., "Wage Determination with Bilateral Monopoly in the

Labour Market: A Theoretical Treatment," *Economic Record, 46* (March 1970), pp. 55-72.

96. Hodd, Michael, "An Empirical Investigation of the Heckscher-Ohlin Theory," *Economica, New Series, 34* (February 1967), pp. 20-29.

97. Hoffmeyer, Erik, "The Leontief Paradox Critically Examined," *Manchester School of Economic and Social Studies, 26* (May 1958), pp. 160-179.

98. Holmes, R. A., and Munro, J. M., "Regional Nonfarm Income Differences in Canada: An Econometric Study," *Journal of Regional Science, 10* (April 1970), pp. 65-74.

99. Hong, Wontack, "The Heckscher-Ohlin Theory of Factor Price Equalization and the Indeterminacy in International Specialization," *International Economic Review, 11* (June 1970), pp. 328-333.

100. Horiba, Y., "A Note on the Factor Proportions Theory in the N-Factor Case," *Kyklos, 24* (Fasc. 2, 1971), pp. 339-343.

101. Inada, K., "Investment in Fixed Capital and Stability of Growth Equilibrium," *Review of Economic Studies, 33* (January 1966), pp. 19-30.

102. Johansen, Leif, "A Note on the Theory of Interindustrial Wage Differentials," *Review of Economic Studies, 25* (February 1958), pp. 109-113.

103. Johnson, D. G., "Labor Mobility and Agricultural Adjustment," in *Agricultural Adjustment Problems in a Growing Economy* (E. O. Heady, H. G. Diesslin, H. R. Jensen and G. L. Johnson, eds.). Ames, Iowa: State College Press, 1958.

104. Johnson, Harry G., "Optimal Trade Intervention in the Presence of Domestic Distortions," in R. Baldwin *et al., Trade Growth and the Balance of Payments* (Richard E. Caves, Harry G. Johnson and Peter B. Kenen, eds.). Amsterdam: North Holland, 1965, pp. 3-34.

105. Johnson, Harry G., "Factor Market Distortions and the Shape of the Transformation Curve," *Econometrica, 34* (July 1966), pp. 686-698.

106. Johnson, Harry G., "Factor Endowments, International Trade, and Factor Prices," reprinted in *A.E.A. Readings in International Economics* (R. E. Caves and H. G. Johnson, eds.). Homewood, Ill.: Richard D. Irwin, 1968, pp. 78-89.

107. Johnson, Harry G., "Minimum Wage Laws: A General Equilibrium Analysis," *Canadian Journal of Economics, 2* (November 1969), pp. 599-604.

108. Johnson, Harry G., *The Two-Sector Model of General Equilibrium.* Chicago: Aldine Press, 1971.

109. Johnson, Harry G., *The Theory of Income Distribution.* London: Gray-Mills Publishing, 1973.

110. Johnson, Harry G., and Mieszkowski, Peter, "The Effects of Unionization on the Distribution of Income: A General Equilibrium Approach," *Quarterly Journal of Economics, 84* (November 1970), pp. 539-561.

111. Jones, Ronald W., "The Structure of Simple General Equilibrium Models," *Journal of Political Economy, 73* (December 1965) pp. 557-572.

112. Jones, Ronald W., "Distortions in Factor Markets and the General Equilibrium Model of Production," *Journal of Political Economy, 79* (May/June 1971), pp. 437-459.

113. Kafka, A., "An Economic Justification of Protectionism: Further Comments," *Quarterly Journal of Economics, 76* (February 1962), pp. 163-166.

114. Katrak, Homi, "An Empirical Test of Comparative Cost Theories: Japan, Peru, The United Kingdom and The United States," *Economica, New Series, 36* (November 1969), pp. 389-399.

115. Keesing, Donald, "Labor Skills and Comparative Advantage," *American Economic Review, 56* (May 1966), pp. 249-258.

116. Kemp, Murray C., "Some Issues in the Analysis of Trade Gains," *Oxford Economic Papers, 20* (July 1968), pp. 149-161.

117. Kemp, Murray C., *The Pure Theory of International Trade and Investment,* Englewood Cliffs, N. J.: Prentice-Hall, 1969.

118. Kemp, Murray C., and Jones, Ronald W., "Variable Labor Supply and the Theory of International Trade," *Journal of Political Economy, 70* (February 1962), pp. 30-36.

119. Kemp, Murray C., and Negishi, T., "Domestic Distortions, Tariffs and the Theory of Optimum Subsidy," *Journal of Political Economy, 77* (November 1969), pp. 1011-1013.

120. Kemp, Murray C., and Negishi, T., "Variable Returns to Scale Commodity Taxes, Factor Market Distortions and Their Implications for Trade Gains," *Swedish Journal of Economics, 72* (June 1970), pp. 1-11.

121. Kenen, P. B., "Development, Mobility and the Case for Tariffs," *Kyklos, 16* (Fasc. 2, 1963), pp. 321-324.

122. Kindleberger, Charles P., *International Economics,* 1st ed. Homewood, Ill.: Richard D. Irwin, 1953.

123. Kindleberger, Charles P., *The Terms of Trade: A European Case Study.* Cambridge, Mass.: MIT Press, 1956.

124. Kleiman, E., "On the Validity of the Leontief Paradox Test," *Kyklos, 20* (Fasc. 3, 1967), pp. 742-746.

125. Koo, A. Y. C., "An Economic Justification for Protectionism: Comment," Quarterly Journal of Economics, 75 (February 1961), pp. 133-144.

126. Kravis, Irving B., "Wages and Foreign Trade," *Review of Economics and Statistics, 38* (February 1956), pp. 14-30.

127. Kreinin, Mordechai, "The Leontief Scarce-Factor Paradox," *American Economic Review, 55* (March 1965), pp. 131-140.

128. Lefeber, Louis, "Trade and Minimum Wage Rates," in *Trade, Balance of Payments and Growth* (J. Bhagwati *et al.*, eds.), Amsterdam: North Holland, 1971.

129. Leontief, Wassily W., "Domestic Production and Foreign Trade: The American Capital Position Re-examined," *Economia Internazionale, 7* (February 1954), pp. 3-32.

130. Leontief, Wassily W., "Factor Proportions and the Structure of American Trade: Further Theoretical and Empirical Analysis," *Review of Economics and Statistics, 38* (November 1956), pp. 386-407.

131. Leontief, Wassily W., "Reply," *Review of Economics and Statistics, 60* (Supplement, February 1958), pp. 119-122.

132. Leontief, Wassily W., "Leontief's Paradox: A Reply," *Review of Economics and Statistics, 49* (November 1967), p. 607.

133. Lester, Richard A., "A Range Theory of Wage Differentials," *Industrial and Labor Relations Review, 5* (July 1952), pp. 483-501.

134. Lewis, H. G., *Unionism and Relative Wages in the United States.* Chicago: University of Chicago Press, 1963.

135. Lewis, W. Arthur, "Economic Development with Unlimited Supplies of Labour," in *The Economics of Underdevelopment* (A. N. Agarwale and S. P. Singh, eds.). New York: Oxford University Press, 1963, pp. 400-449. Reprinted from *The Manchester School, 22* (May 1954), pp. 139-191.

136. Linder, Staffan Burenstam, *An Essay on Trade and Transformation.* New York: Wiley, 1961, pp. 76-78.

137. Lloyd, P. J., "The Shape of the Transformation Curve With and Without Factor Market Distortions," *Australian Economic Papers, 9* (June 1970), pp. 52-61.

138. Locks, Mitchell O., "The Influence of Pattern-Bargaining on Manufacturing Wages in the Cleveland, Ohio, Labor Market, 1945-1950," *Review of Economics and Statistics, 37* (February 1955), pp. 70-76.

139. Lurie, Melvin, "The Effect of Unionization on Wages in the Transit Industry," *Journal of Political Economy, 69* (December 1961), pp. 558-572.

140. Magee, Stephen P., "Factor Market Distortions and the Pure Theory of International Trade," unpublished Ph.D. dissertation. Cambridge, Mass.: Massachusetts, Institute of Technology, May 1969.

141. Magee, Stephen P., "Factor Market Distortions, Production, Distribution and the Pure Theory of International Trade," *Quarterly Journal of Economics, 75* (November 1971), pp. 623-643.

142. Magee, Stephen P., "Factor Market Distortions and Empirical Tests of the Heckscher-Ohlin Theorem," Report 7213. Chicago: Center for Mathematical Studies in Business and Economics, University of Chicago, 1972.

143. Magee, Stephen P., "A Geometric Note on the Derivation of the Production Possibility Curve and the Shrinkage Effect of Factor Market Distortions," unpublished, University of Chicago, August 1972.

144. Magee, Stephen P., "Factor Market Distortions, Production, and Trade: A Survey," *Oxford Economic Papers, 25* (March 1973), pp. 1-43.

145. Maher, J. E., "Union, Nonunion Wage Differentials," *American Economic Review, 46* (June 1956), pp. 336-352.

146. Manoilesco, Mihail, *The Theory of Protection and International Trade.* London: P. S. King and Son, Ltd., 1931.

147. Mansfield, Edwin, "Wage Differentials in the Cotton Textile Industry, 1933-1952," *Review of Economics and Statistics, 37* (February 1955), pp. 77-82.

148. Marquez-Ruarte, Jorge, "An Elementary Framework for Inter-Run Analysis," paper presented at the International Economics Workshop, University of Chicago, March 1973.

149. Marx, Daniel, "Regulation of International Liner Shipping and 'Freedom of the Seas,' " *Journal of Industrial Economics, 16* (November 1967), pp. 46-62.

150. Mayer, Wolfgang, "Short-Run and Long-Run Equilibrium for a Small Open Economy," *Journal of Political Economy, 82* (September/ October 1974), pp. 955-967.

151. McCormick, B. J., and E. Owen Smith, *The Labour Market.* Baltimore: Penguin, 1968.

152. McGuire, Timothy W., and Rapping, Leonard A., "The Supply of Labor and Manufacturing Wage Determination in the United States: An Empirical Examination," *International Economic Review, 11* (June 1970), pp. 258-268.

153. McLean, A. A., "Selective Employment Tax: Impact on Prices and the Balance of Payments," *Scottish Journal of Political Economy, 17* (February 1970), pp. 1-17.

154. Meade, J. E., *Trade and Welfare*. London: Oxford University Press, 1955.

155. Meier, Gerald M., "Free Trade and Development Economics," in *Value, Capital and Growth: Papers in Honor of Sir John Hicks* (J. N. Wolfe, ed.). Edinburgh: University of Edinburgh Press, 1968, pp. 385-414.

156. Mendelsohn, Chaim, "A Theoretical Framework for Analysis of Some Contemporary Problems of International Trade in Agricultural Products," *Journal of Farm Economics, 39* (December 1957), pp. 1724-1731.

157. Merrett, S. R., "The Leontief Paradox," *Economic Journal, 75* (September 1965), p. 641.

158. Metzler, Lloyd A., "Tariffs, the Terms of Trade, and the Distribution of National Income," in *A.E.A. Readings in International Economics* (R. E. Caves and H. G. Johnson, eds.). Homewood, Ill.: Richard D. Irwin, 1968, pp. 24-57.

159. Meyers, F., "Price Theory and Union Monopoly: Reply," *Industrial and Labor Relations Review, 13* (October 1959), pp. 94-95.

160. Michaely, M., "Factor Proportions in International Trade: Current State of the Theory," *Kyklos, 17* (Fasc. 4, 1964), pp. 529-550.

161. Mieszkowski, P. M., "On the Theory of Tax Incidence," *Journal of Political Economy, 75* (June 1967), pp. 250-262.

162. Miller, Norman C., "Factor Market Imperfections, Increasing Marginal Returns, and Optimum Input Proportions," *Southern Economic Journal, 37* (October 1970), pp. 205-208.

163. Minabe, Nobuo, "The Heckscher-Ohlin Theorem, the Leontief Paradox, and Patterns of Economic Growth," *American Economic Review, 56* (December 1966), pp. 1193-1211.

164. Mincer, Jacob, "The Distribution of Labor Incomes: A Survey with Special Reference to the Human Capital Approach," *Journal of Economic LIterature, 8* (March 1970), pp. 1-26.

165. Minhas, Bagicha S., *An International Comparison of Factor Costs and Factor Use*. Amsterdam: North Holland, 1963.

166. Mishan, E. J., and L. Needleman, "Immigration, Excess Aggregate Demand and the Balance of Payments," *Economica, New Series, 33* (May 1966), pp. 129-147.

167. Mitchell, Daniel J. B., *Essays on Labor and International Trade*. Los Angeles: University of California, Institute of Industrial Relations, 1970.

168. Mitchell, Edward J., "Explaining the International Pattern of Labor

Productivity and Wages: A Production Model with Two Labor Inputs," *Review of Economics and Statistics, 50* (November 1968), pp. 461-469.

169. Moroney, John R., "Factor Prices, Factor Proportions, and Regional Factor Endowments," *Journal of Political Economy, 78* (February 1970), pp. 158-164.

170. Moroney, John R., and Walker, James M., "A Regional Test of the Heckscher-Ohlin Hypothesis," *Journal of Political Economy, 74* (December 1966), pp. 573-586.

171. Mundell, Robert A., "International Trade and Factor Mobility," *A.E.A. Readings in International Economics* (R. E. Caves and H. G. Johnson, eds.). Homewood, Ill.: Richard D. Irwin, 1968, pp. 101-114.

172. Mundlak, Yair, "Further Implications of Distortion in the Factor Market," *Econometrica, 38* (May 1970), pp. 517-532.

173. Myint, H., "Protection and Economic Development," in *International Trade Theory in a Developing World* (R. Harrod and D. C. Hague, eds.). London: Macmillan, 1963.

174. Myint, H., *The Economics of Developing Countries.* London: Hutchinson University Library, 1967.

175. Ohlin, Bertil, "Protection and Non-Competing Groups," *Weltwirtschaftliches Archiv, 33* (Heft 1, 1931), pp. 30-45.

176. Ohlin, Bertil, *Interregional and International Trade.* Cambridge, Mass.: Harvard University Press, 1933.

177. Odaka, K., "Rationalizing Intra-Industry Wage Differentials: An Analytical Framework," *Hitotsubashi Journal of Economics, 7* (June 1966), pp. 80-99.

178. Oniki, H., and Uzawa, H., "Patterns of Trade and Investment in a Dynamic Model of International Trade," *Review of Economic Studies, 32* (January 1965), pp. 15-38.

179. Ozanne, Robert, "A Century of Occupational Differentials in Manufacturing," *Review of Economics and Statistics, 44* (August 1962), pp. 292-299.

180. Papola, T. S., and Bharadwaj, V. P., "Dynamics of Industrial Wage Structure: An Inter-Country Analysis," *Economic Journal, 80* (March 1970), pp. 72-90.

181. Parker, John E., and Burton, John F., "Volunteer Labor Mobility in the U. S. Manufacturing Sector," in *Proceedings of the Twentieth Annual Winter Meeting* (Gerald G. Somers, ed.). Industrial Relations Research Association, 1968, pp. 61-70. Reprinted in John F. Burton, Jr., Lee K. Benham, William M. Vaugh III, and Robert J. Flanagan, *Readings in*

*Labor Market Analysis.* New York: Holt, Rinehart and Winston, 1971.

182. Peitchinis, S. G., "Occupational Wage Differentials in Canada, 1939-1965," *Australian Economic Papers, 8* (June 1969), pp. 20-40.

183. Perlman, R., "A Note on the Measurement of Real Wage Differentials," *Review of Economics and Statistics, 41* (May 1959), pp. 192-195.

184. Pierson, Gail, "The Effect of Union Strength on the U. S. 'Phillips Curve,'" *American Economic Review, 58* (June 1968), pp. 456-467.

185. Ramaswami, V. K., "International Factor Movement and the National Advantage," *Economica, 35* (August 1968), pp. 305-327.

186. Ramaswami, V. K., "Welfare Maximization When Domestic Factor Movement Entails External Diseconomies," *Journal of Political Economy, 78* (September/October 1970), pp. 1061-1068.

187. Ramaswami, V. K., *Trade and Development: Essays and Economics,* Cambridge, Mass.: MIT Press, 1972.

188. Ramaswami, V. K., and Srinivasan, Key N., "Optimal Subsidies and Taxes When Some Factors Are Traded," *Journal of Political Economy, 76* (July/August 1968), pp. 569-582.

189. Reder, Melvin W., "The Theory of Occupational Wage Differences," *American Economic Review, 45* (December 1955), pp. 833-852.

190. Reder, Melvin W., "Wage Differentials: Theory and Measurement," in *Aspects of Labor Economics.* New York: National Bureau of Economic Research, 1962, pp. 257-299. Reprinted in John F. Burton, Jr., Lee K. Benham, William M. Vaugh III, and Robert J. Flanagan, *Readings in Labor Market Analysis.* New York: Holt, Rinehart and Winston, 1971.

191. Robinson, Joan, *The Economics of Imperfect Competition.* London: Macmillan, 1934.

192. Robinson, Romney, "Factor Proportions and Comparative Advantage," *Quarterly Journal of Economics, 70* (May 1956), pp. 169-192.

193. Robinson, Romney, "Comment," *Review of Economics and Statistics, 60* (Supplement, February 1958), pp. 113-116.

194. Rodriguez, Carlos A., "Aspects of International Factor Mobility," unpublished Ph.D. dissertation. Chicago: Department of Economics, University of Chicago, 1973.

195. Ross, A. M., and Goldner, W., "Forces Affecting the Interindustry Wage Structure," *Quarterly Journal of Economics, 64* (May 1950), pp. 254-281.

196. Rybczynski, T. M., "Factor Endowment and Relative Commodity Prices," in *A.E.A. Readings in International Economics* (R. E. Caves and H. G. Johnson, eds.). Homewood, Ill.: Richard D. Irwin, 1968, pp. 72-77.

197. Salant, Walter S., "The Balance of Payments Deficit and the Tax Structure," *Review of Economics and Statistics, 46* (May 1964), pp. 131-138.

198. Samuelson, M. C., "The Australian Case for Protection Re-examined," *Quarterly Journal of Economics, 54* (November 1939), pp. 148-149.

199. Samuelson, Paul A., *Foundations of Economic Analysis.* Cambridge, Mass.: Harvard University Press, 1947, Chap. VIII.

200. Samuelson, Paul A., "International Factor-Price Equalizations Once Again," in *A.E.A. Readings in International Economics* (R. E. Caves and H. G. Johnson, eds.). Homewood, Ill.: Richard D. Irwin, 1968, pp. 58-71.

201. Samuelson, Paul A., "Theoretical Notes on Trade Problems," *Review of Economics and Statistics, 46* (May 1964), pp. 145-154.

202. Sawhney, P. K., "Inter-industry Wage Differentials in India," *Indian Economic Journal, 17* (August/September 1969), pp. 28-56.

203. Savosnick, K. M., "The Box Diagram and the Production Possibility Curve," *Ekonomisk Tidskrift, 60* (September 1958), pp. 183-197.

204. Schlesinger, J. R., "Market Structure, Union Power and Inflation," *Southern Economic Journal, 24* (January 1958), pp. 296-312.

205. Schwartz, Eli, "A Note on Wage Structures and Foreign Trade," *Weltwirtschaftliches Archiv, 83* (Heft 2, 1959), pp. 250-252.

206. Schwartzman, David, "The Effect of Monopoly on Price," *Journal of Political Economy, 67* (August 1959), pp. 352-362.

207. Schwartzman, David, "Monopoly and Wages," *Canadian Journal of Economics and Political Science, 26* (August 1960), pp. 428-438.

208. Segal, M., "Regional Wage Differences in Manufacturing," *Review of Economics and Statistics, 43* (May 1961), pp. 148-155.

209. Segal, M., "The Relation Between Union Wage Impact and Market Structure," *Quarterly Journal of Economics, 78* (February 1964), pp. 96-114.

210. Shepherd, William G., "Trends of Concentration in American Manufacturing Industries, 1947-1958," *Review of Economics and Statistics, 46* (May 1964), pp. 200-212.

211. Simler, N. J., "Unionism and Labor's Share in Manufacturing Industries," *Review of Economics and Statistics, 43* (November 1961), pp. 369-378.

212. Sjaastad, Larry A., "The Costs and Returns of Human Migration," *Journal of Political Economy, 70* (Supplement October 1962), pp. 80-93. Reprinted in John F. Burton, Jr., Lee K. Benham, William M. Vaugh III, and Robert J. Flanagan, *Readings in Labor Market Analysis.* New York: Holt, Rinehart and Winston, 1971.

213. Stafford, Frank, "Concentration and Labor Earnings; Comment," *American Economic Review, 58* (March 1968), pp. 174-181.
214. *Statistical Abstract of the United States, 1974,* 95th ed. Washington, D.C.: U. S. Government Printing Office, 1974.
215. Stigler, George J., "Imperfections in the Capital Market," *Journal of Political Economy, 75* (June 1967), pp. 287-292.
216. Stolper, Wolfgang F., and Roskamp, K. W., "An Input-Output Table for West Germany with Applications to Foreign Trade," *Bulletin of the Oxford Institute of Economics and Statistics, 23* (November 1961), pp. 379-392.
217. Stolper, W., and Samuelson, P. A., "Protection and Real Wages," *The Review of Economic Studies, 9* (November 1941), pp. 58-63.
218. Sultan, Paul E., "Unionism and Wage-Income Ratios: 1929-1951," *The Review of Economics and Statistics, 36* (November 1954), pp. 67-73.
219. Swerling, Boris C., "Capital Shortage and Labor Surplus in the United States?" *Review of Economics and Statistics, 36* (August 1954), pp. 286-289.
220. Tarshis, Lorie, "Factor Inputs and International Price Comparisons," in *The Allocation of Economic Resources* (M. Abramovitz *et al.,* eds.). Stanford, Calif.: Stanford University Press, 1959, pp. 236-244.
221. Tatemoto, Masahiro, and Ichimura, Shinichi, "Factor Proportions and Foreign Trade: The Case of Japan," *Review of Economics and Statistics, 41* (November 1959), pp. 442-446.
222. Taussig, F., *International Trade.* New York: Macmillan, 1927, pp. 43-60.
223. Taylor, David P., "Discrimination and Occupational Wage Differences in the Market for Unskilled Labor," *Industrial and Labor Relations Review, 21* (April 1968), pp. 375-390. Reprinted in John F. Burton, Jr., Lee K. Benham, William M. Vaugh III, and Robert J. Flanagan, *Readings in Labor Market Analysis.* New York: Holt, Rinehart and Winston, 1971.
224. Throop, A. W., "The Union-Nonunion Wage Differential and Cost-Push Inflation," *American Economic Review, 58* (March 1968), pp. 79-99.
225. Uekawa, Y., "On a Two-Sector Growth Model with Non-Shiftable Capital," unpublished, 1970.
226. Ulman, L., "Marshall and Friedman on Union Strength," *Review of Economics and Statistics, 37* (November 1955), pp. 384-406. Reprinted in John F. Burton, Jr., Lee K. Benham, William M. Vaugh III, and Robert J. Flanagan, *Readings in Labor Market Analysis.* New York: Holt, Rinehart and Winston, 1971.

227. Utsumi, Y., "Rigidity of Wage Rate and the Interfirm Wage Differentials," *Osaka Economic Papers, 6* (February 1958), pp. 39-58.
228. Vacara, Beatrice, "Comment," *Review of Economics and Statistics, 60* (Supplement, February 1958), pp. 118-119.
229. Valavanis-Vail, Stefan, "Leontief's Scarce Factor Paradox," *Journal of Political Economy, 62* (December 1954), pp. 523-528.
230. Valavanis-Vail, Stefan, "Comment," *Review of Economics and Statistics, 60* (Supplement, February 1958), pp. 111-113.
231. Vanderkamp, John, "Migration Flows, Their Determinants and the Effects of Return Migration," *Journal of Political Economy, 79* (September/October 1971), pp. 1012-1031.
232. Vanek, J., "The Factor Proportions Theory: A N-Factor Case," *Kyklos, 21* (Fasc. 4, 1968), pp. 749-756.
233. Vanek, J., and Bertrand, T. J., "Trade and Factor Prices in a Multi-Commodity World," in *Trade, Balance of Payments and Growth* (J. Bhagwati *et al.,* eds.). Amsterdam: North Holland, 1971, pp. 49-65.
234. Vernon, Raymond, "International Investment and International Trade in the Product Cycle," *Quarterly Journal of Economics, 80* (May 1966), pp. 190-207.
235. Viner, Jacob, "The Theory of Protection and International Trade: A Review," *Journal of Political Economy, 40* (February 1932), pp. 121-125.
236. Viner, Jacob, *International Trade and Economic Development.* Oxford: Oxford University Press, 1953.
237. Viner, Jacob, *Studies in the Theory of International Trade.* London: George Allen and Unwin, reprinted, 1964, pp. 453-462, 493-500.
238. Wahl, Donald F., "Capital and Labour Requirements for Canada's Foreign Trade," *Canadian Journal of Economics and Political Science, 27* (August 1961), pp. 349-358.
239. Webb, L. Roy, "International Factor Movement and the National Advantage: A Comment," *Economica, 37* (February 1970), pp. 81-84.
240. Weinstein, P. A., "Featherbedding: A Theoretical Analysis," Journal of *Political Economy, 68* (August 1960), pp. 379-387.
241. Weiser, Lawrence A., "Changing Factor Requirements of United States Foreign Trade," *Review of Economics and Statistics, 50* (August 1968), pp. 356-360.
242. Weiss, Leonard, "Concentration and Labor Earnings," *American Economic Review, 56* (March 1966), pp. 96-117. Reprinted in John F. Burton, Jr., Lee K. Benham, William M. Vaugh III, and Robert J. Flanagan, *Readings in Labor Market Analysis.* New York: Holt, Rinehart and Winston, 1971.

243. Wolfson, R. J., "An Econometric Investigation of Regional Differences in American Agricultural Wages," *Econometrica, 26* (April 1958), pp. 225-257.
244. Yeh, Y., "A Note on Domestic Distortions and the Terms of Trade," *Economica, New Series, 33* (August 1966), pp. 341-344.

# Author Index

Numbers in brackets are reference numbers and indicate that an author's work is referred to although his name is not cited in the text.

# Subject Index

## A

Abundant factor, 66, 111
Actor guilds, 45
Adjustment process, 85-86
Aggregate demand, 93
Agricultural sector, 55, 75
Autarky, 79, 82

## B

Balance of payments equilibrium,
    defined, 21
Bilateral monopoly, 85
Budget line, 20
Business cycle, 88

## C

Capital:
  defined, 15
  immobility of, 86
  international cross-flows of, 75, 111
  mobility of, 73-74

[Capital]
  taxation of, 103
Capital-labor ratios, 33, 65, 106-
    108
Case i, 33, 66
  defined, 25-26
Case ii, 34, 66
  defined, 25-26
Cleveland, Ohio, labor market, 89
Closed economy, 95-103, 111
Cobb-Douglas production functions,
    40, 58, 95, 109, 111-112
Cobb-Douglas utility functions, 95,
    111
Commodity subsidy, 103
Commodity taxes, 111, 112
Community indifference curves, 69,
    83
Comparative advantage, 11-13,
    65-72 (*see also* Trade)
Comparative statics, 25
Complete specialization, 107
Concentrated industries, 90
Consumer demand, 19